A Phot

BIRDS
OF PREY
OF SOUTHERN, CENTRAL
AND EAST AFRICA

David Allan

First published in 1996 by
New Holland (Publishers) Ltd
London • Cape Town • Sydney • Singapore

24 Nutford Place
London W1H 6DQ
United Kingdom

80 McKenzie Street
Cape Town 8001
South Africa

3/2 Aquatic Drive
Frenchs Forest, NSW 2086
Australia

ISBN 185368 9033

Editor: Helena Reid
Managing Editor: Pippa Parker
Designer: Damian Gibbs
Design Manager: Odette Marais
Cartography: Lyndall Hamilton
Illustrations: Peter Hayman

Reproduction by cmyk Prepress
Printed and bound in Singapore by Tien Wah Press (Pte) Ltd

Front cover: Fish Eagle (Daryl Balfour)
Spine: Barn Owl (S.C. Hendriks)
Back cover: Bateleur (Nigel Dennis, ABPL)
Title page: White-headed Vulture (M.C. Wilkes, Aquila)

Contents

Key to thumbnail outlines

Harrier	*Vulture*	*Kite*	*Falcon*
Eagle	*Buzzard*	*Hawk*	*Owl*

Introduction

Birds of prey are arguably the most impressive and exciting of all forms of wildlife. Their haughty demeanour and rapacious habits lend them an aura unparalleled by other birds. They also provide the ultimate test of identification skills for the bird-watcher. Recent advances in our knowledge have revolutionized our ability to meet these identification challenges. This photoguide provides detailed texts, distribution maps, colour photographs and illustrations to synthesize the most up-to-date information available on African raptor identification. Sadly, many birds of prey are threatened in the modern world and hopefully our increased familiarity with these magnificent birds will translate into an ever stronger determination to ensure their survival.

Identifying birds of prey – the problems

There are several reasons why African birds of prey are difficult to identify. One is the diversity of species: 83 diurnal raptors and 19 owls occur in the region covered by this guide, that is southern (South Africa, Namibia, Botswana, Zimbabwe, southern Mozambique, Lesotho, Swaziland), central (Zambia, Malawi, northern Mozambique) and east (Kenya, Tanzania, Uganda) Africa. Another reason is that these shy birds rarely allow a close approach. Immature plumages, which are typically different from those of adults, also present difficulties. Immatures are normally browner than adults, their upperparts are tipped buff, giving a 'scaled' appearance to the back, and the colours of their eyes and exposed skin on the cere, head, neck and legs frequently change between immaturity and adulthood.

Males and females can also differ, as seen in the harriers and kestrels, and some species show different colour forms or 'morphs'. These may involve pale and dark forms (for example, the Wahlberg's and Booted eagles), grey and rufous forms (for example the Common Scops and Spotted Eagle owls), and all-black 'melanistic' plumages (for example, the Ovambo and Black sparrowhawks and the Gabar and African goshawks). Some raptors, especially the 'brown' eagles and buzzards, show variation in the shades of brown in the plumage and the extent of underlying markings.

Identifying birds of prey – the solutions

Since raptors rarely allow a leisurely examination it is essential to study guides such as this before venturing out into the field. Observers should take note of the key identification features beforehand, so that these can be looked for quickly before the bird slips out of view.

The first area to be mastered in identifying birds of prey is the differentiation between the major groups of raptors:

Vultures are large to very large raptors. Their wings are long, broad, and well suited to their soaring flight. They subsist on carrion. Their beaks are powerful, allowing them to tear through the thick skin of large dead mammals but since they do not kill their own prey, their feet and talons are less powerful than those of other raptors. Their bare heads and necks are adaptations for their carrion-eating habits. They are social birds which often congregate in large numbers around carcasses, and often roost, bathe and breed communally. When perched, most vultures can easily be identified at close range. Since they are highly aerial birds the challenge, however, is to identify them in flight by their shape, size and underwing markings. The heads and necks of most vultures appear small and narrow in flight; a useful feature in differentiating flying vultures from other large birds of prey (nine species).

Eagles are medium-sized to very large raptors. Despite their reputation for being large, the smaller eagles are about the same size as buzzards. Their wings are long, broad and adapted for soaring flight. Unlike other diurnal raptors, some eagles have feathered legs down to their feet. This feature is shared by the *Aquila* and 'hawk eagles' (the Long-crested, Black, Tawny, Steppe, Eastern Imperial, Lesser Spotted, Greater Spotted, Wahlberg's, Booted, Martial, Crowned, African Hawk and Ayres' eagles). The four snake eagles and the Bateleur and African Fish eagles, however, have bare unfeathered legs and feet. The majority of eagles are solitary birds, except for the migratory Steppe, Lesser Spotted and Greater Spotted eagles, and are found alone or in pairs. Most of the identification problems associated with this group involve the numerous 'brown' eagles, the ranks of which are bolstered by brown immatures that have distinctive black-and-white plumages as adults (19 species).

Kites are small to medium-sized raptors. The Common Black-shouldered and African Swallow-tailed kites are distinctive and differ from the more typical and medium-sized Black Kite. All three species, however, share the same wing shape in flight with the wing bending backwards at the carpal joint, midway along the wing. The Swallow-tailed and Black kites are highly aerial with a leisurely flight action. Most kites feed on carrion and other waste, and are associated with regions with dense human populations. The Black-shouldered and Swallow-tailed kites, however, feed solely on live prey. Kites are social birds and congregate in large numbers at food. All kites tend to roost communally (three species).

Harriers are medium-sized raptors. They have a round facial disk, similar to that found in owls. This adaptation enables them to hear the scurrying of small animals on the ground. They have long narrow wings and tails, and long legs. Harriers forage by coursing slowly just above the ground. When they spot small animals, they execute a backwards roll-pounce onto their prey. They live in flat, open areas and wetlands. The males and females of most species differ in appearance (five species).

Buzzards are medium-sized, stocky raptors with relatively large heads, and short legs and tails. Their wings are long and broad, and they soar well. They hunt from tall perches and frequently perch on roadside telephone poles. Buzzards show substantial variation in plumage colour and pattern (seven species).

Sparrowhawks and *goshawks* are small to medium-sized raptors. They typically have fine barring on the underparts. Their heads are relatively small, their wings are short, broad and round, and their tails are long. When perched, the tips of their wings stop well short of the tips of their tails. Their shape is an adaptation allowing manœuvrability when darting through closed forest and dense woodland (habitats most favoured by these secretive species). Some species overlap in size, and the females are markedly larger than the males. Size, the pattern on the upper surface of the tail and the rump, the precise pattern of markings on the underparts, and the colours of the soft parts are useful identification features. Some species have all-black melanistic forms. The two chanting goshawks differ from the other sparrowhawks and goshawks. They are sluggish in habits and live in fairly open environments. The Lizard Buzzard is closely related to the chanting goshawks and should be included in this group rather than with the true buzzards (12 species).

Falcons and *kestrels* are small to medium-sized raptors. They have large heads and their wings are long, narrow and pointed. When perched, the tips of their wings extend to the tips of their tails. Their wing shape is an adaptation for fast, direct flight, and plunging stoops in the open environments they favour. A common facial feature is a dark moustachial stripe extending downwards from the eye. The males and females of some kestrels are markedly different. Most of the kestrels hover when hunting and some forage and roost in large flocks. Falcons and kestrels do not build their own nests and lay their eggs on cliff ledges and in trees in the disused nests of other birds (18 species).

Owls have large heads, often with distinctive ear-tufts, and stocky bodies. Their faces are dominated by their large eyes. The round, flat facial disk enhances binocular vision, an essential adaptation for judging distance in the twilight, and also channels sound into their sensitive ears. Owls are nocturnal but several species are active during dusk and dawn. They do not build their own nests and they lay their eggs on the ground, in holes and cavities in trees and cliffs, and in the disused nests of other birds. There are no significant differences between the appearance of adults and immatures or between males and females, and most species are easily identified. Two species (Common Scops and Spotted Eagle owls) have two different colour forms. Key features in identifying owls include size, plumage colour, the presence or absence of ear-tufts, eye colour and the pattern of markings on the under- and upperparts. Owls are usually heard rather than seen and knowledge of their calls is therefore crucial (12 species).

After mastering the major groups, it is important to also take note of the distribution, migration patterns and calls of birds of prey in order to accurately identify the different species. Distribution is useful in identification since many similar species show no, or only slight, overlap in range (for example, the Pale and Dark Chanting goshawks). The habitat favoured by each raptor often reveals its identity. Forest Buzzards, for example, are restricted to forests, while Steppe Buzzards typically occur in both open and forested areas.

Knowledge of the migration patterns of raptors is important, as observers should not expect to see a species during the period when it has moved north of our region. Twenty species are non-breeding migrants and only occur in the region covered by this guide during the period late October to late March. They are the Steppe, Eastern Imperial, Lesser Spotted and Greater Spotted eagles, Black Kite, European Marsh, Montagu's and Pallid harriers, Steppe, Long-legged, Honey and Grasshopper buzzards, European and Sparrowhawk, Saker, Sooty, Eleonora's, Eastern Red-footed and Western Red-footed falcons, European Hobby, and Lesser Kestrel. An additional two raptors (Wahlberg's Eagle and the yellow-billed race of the Black Kite) are breeding migrants present between August and March. The Osprey is also a migrant but many immature birds remain in the region during our winter.

The calls of the diurnal raptors are of little value in identification. Most of these species are largely silent and their calls are simple and stereotyped. The calls of the noisier species, however, can be useful in identificaiton, or at least in drawing the observer's attention to the presence of these birds (for example, the 'clicking' note of the African Goshawk). By contrast, the calls of owls are invaluable in identification and hearing them is the most common way of encountering these nocturnal predators. Cassette tapes of recorded bird calls can be used to become familiar with the calls of the various owls. The best collection of African recordings is found in Guy Gibbon's (1991) *Southern African Bird Sounds*, available from Southern African Birding, P.O. Box 24106, Hillary 4024, South Africa.

Where to find birds of prey

The best places to find birds of prey are national parks and nature reserves. This is due to ease of access and because many African raptors' numbers, especially those of vultures and larger eagles, have decreased outside of protected and uninhabited areas. Many of Africa's most renowned protected areas comprise flat open woodland, a habitat which offers the highest diversity and number of large raptors.

Many other areas, however, still support diverse assemblages of raptors, including many species that are usually rare or absent on the plains of the larger woodland reserves. Many birds of prey are attracted to cliffs for breeding and several species have wing shapes adapted to exploiting the winds associated with mountainous regions. Mountain specialists include the Bearded Vulture, Black Eagle, Peregrine and Taita falcons, and the Cape Eagle Owl. The other cliff-nesting raptors are the Cape and Rüppell's vultures, Booted Eagle, Jackal and Augur buzzards, Gymnogene, Lanner Falcon and Rock Kestrel. Cliffs within the ranges of these species should be searched for their presence. Clues to their occupancy include 'whitewash' from the birds' droppings and the presence of nests.

Forests also support a suite of raptors dependent on this habitat. These include the Bat Hawk, Long-crested, Crowned and Southern Banded Snake eagles, Forest Buzzard, Cuckoo Hawk, African Goshawk, Little and Black sparrowhawks, and African Wood and African Barred owls. Many forest raptors, especially the sparrowhawks and goshawks, have adapted to using plantations of alien trees. As a general rule, the localities with the tallest trees, typically along watercourses, are good places for locating raptors.

Several birds of prey can be classed as waterbirds, and major wetlands and rivers should be scoured for these species. This group comprises the African Fish Eagle, Osprey, African and European marsh harriers, and the Marsh, African Grass and Pel's Fishing owls.

African raptors, however, are not just concentrated in moist habitats such as forests and wetlands. Several species are adapted to desert-like conditions and are numerous in the arid southwest and northeast of the region. They include the Pale Chanting Goshawk, Red-necked and Pygmy falcons, and the Greater Kestrel.

Raptors that feed on birds typically wait in ambush close to places where their prey come to feed, and especially, to drink. Waterpoints in arid regions are therefore particularly fruitful sites for raptors. Red-billed Quelea roosts and, particularly, breeding colonies attract a large number and diversity of birds of prey. So too can termite emergences and locust outbreaks. Observers should note alarm calls and panicky flight in birds, as these are usually caused by the proximity of a hunting raptor. Small birds will also gather to harass a perched raptor, giving hissing calls while doing so. Owls are often singled out for this treatment when small birds locate them during the day. Observers should be alert to such 'mobbing' behaviour; but beware as snakes are also sometimes mobbed in the same manner!

The conservation of birds of prey

Many raptors are threatened, including several of the species discussed in this guide. Eight raptor species occurring in the region are of conservation concern globally and therefore are most at risk. They are the Cape Vulture, Eastern Imperial, Greater Spotted and Southern Banded Snake eagles, Black and Pallid harriers, Taita Falcon, and the Lesser Kestrel.

The threats facing raptors are myriad. They include habitat destruction, such as deforestation, woodland clearing and wetland degradation. The precarious position of the Southern Banded Snake Eagle can be attributed to the devastation of coastal forest, and the decreasing numbers of the African Marsh Harrier are a result of the destruction of wetlands. Pel's Fishing Owl has been hard-hit by the drying of lowland rivers, due to afforestation, damming and irrigation.

One of the greatest threats to raptors comes from the irresponsible use of poisons. Strychnine and other poisons, aimed at controlling mammalian predators, and the spraying of Red-billed Quelea colonies and roosts with toxins result in the killing of large numbers of birds of prey. The scavenging species, such as vultures and some of the larger eagles, are particularly vulnerable to poisoning, and many of these species have now disappeared from large parts of their former ranges. Poisoning also stems from the excessive use of insecticides, the decrease in the number of Lanner Falcons in southern Africa having been attributed to agricultural poisons. Other conservation problems include electrocution by, and collisions with, electricity lines, shooting, the killing of raptors to use their body parts in traditional medicine, drowning in farm reservoirs and, relevant to owls, collisions with motor vehicles and entanglement in fences.

How to use this book

This easy-to-use photoguide focuses on the most typical raptors of the region, covering 88 of the 102 species recorded in southern, central and east Africa. Of these 88 species 76 are diurnal raptors and 12 are owls. The 14 species not dealt with here are all extremely rare or highly localized and are unlikely to be encountered by the casual traveller in the region.

The species accounts are not presented in strict taxonomic order but rather in such a way that the most similar and easily confused pecies are grouped together, to allow direct comparisons between them. The accounts are accompanied by colour photographs, colour illustrations and distribution maps. Colour-coded thumbnail outlines offer the reader easy access to the major groups of raptors.

The species accounts are headed by the common name, the scientific name, the Roberts' number (for species present in southern Africa) and the length from the tip of the bill to the tip of the tail of each bird. Alternative common names appear in the index. Each account focuses on the key identification features; diagnostic features are presented in italics. Variation associated with sex, age and colour forms is discussed. Additional information provided in the accounts includes the abundance and habitat of each species, its migratory patterns, call, breeding habits, favourite localities, its prey and hunting techniques, and relevant taxonomic information.

Photographs have been selected to show the variation associated with age, sex and colour form in each species, both perched and in flight. Colour illustrations are provided to further aid identification by focusing on in flight positions, both from above and below.

The maps show the distribution of each species. The ranges of raptors are well known in southern Africa and Kenya, and any sightings beyond the illustrated distributions in these regions are unlikely. Raptor distributions have been less precisely determined in the rest of east and central Africa, and the ranges shown in this guide for these regions should be regarded with caution. Where a species is known to wander outside its normal distribution this is mentioned in the account.

BODY PARTS OF BIRDS OF PREY

Palm-nut Vulture *Gypohierax angolensis* (147) L 60 cm

This vulture has a bare pink face, heavy pale bill, and black-and-white plumage. In flight it shows short, rounded wings and a *short black tail with a broad white tip*. The underparts and underwing coverts are white, the secondaries are black, and the *primaries are diagnostic, being white with black tips*. The immature vulture is all-brown and can best be identified by its shape, and bare yellow or orange facial skin. In flight the underwing of the immature shows a broad, pale line between the underwing coverts and the flight feathers. The Palm-nut Vulture is unique in that, unlike other vultures, its diet consists mainly of plant matter. It feeds on the fruit of oil palms in which it also nests from May until September. In southern Africa, this vulture is largely restricted to the coasts of northern KwaZulu-Natal and southern Mozambique, but it is more widespread further north in Africa. Vagrants occasionally wander far from the places where this species is usually found. For example, there are several recent records of Palm-nut Vultures scavenging on dead fish along the coast of the Western Cape. In southern Africa, this vulture is most easily seen in KwaZulu-Natal at the Mtunzini palm historical monument site, and at Kosi Bay.

Adult

Sub-adult

Immature

Adult   *Sub-adult*   *Immature*

NICO MYBURGH

Adult

DAVE RICHARDS

Immature

11

Bearded Vulture *Gypaetus barbatus* (119) L 104 cm

The adult is unmistakable due to its large size, its pale, heavily feathered head and neck, black mask and chin tuft, distinctive pale streaks on the upper parts, and its rufous underparts. The immature usually has a black head and neck, paler and often mottled upperparts, and darker underparts. In flight the large size, long narrow pointed wings, and *long diamond-shaped tail* are diagnostic. Seen high overhead, this species resembles a large falcon in shape and shows underwing coverts that are darker than the silver-tinged flight feathers. When viewed from the side, the flight action resembles that of an albatross; the wings are held flat or droop slightly downwards. The immature is noticeably broader winged in flight than the adult; the longer flight feathers are replaced with shorter ones as the bird grows older. The immature Egyptian Vulture (*see* page 14) has a similar tail shape, but is smaller with a narrower head, bill and neck. This vulture is restricted to high mountains in southern and east Africa. It was once more widespread in southern Africa, extending south as far as Cape Town, but is now restricted to the Drakensberg Mountains of Lesotho, and the adjacent areas of KwaZulu-Natal and the Eastern Cape. In southern Africa, this scarce resident can best be viewed during winter at the vulture hide in the Giant's Castle Game Reserve in KwaZulu-Natal. It feeds on bone fragments and shatters large bones by dropping them on favourite rocks. Bearded Vultures nest in deep potholes in tall cliffs from May until July in southern Africa and from January until July in east Africa.

Adult

Immature

Adult

W S CLARK

12

Adult

NIGEL DENNIS

Immature

JOHN CARLYON

13

Egyptian Vulture *Neophron percnopterus* (120) L 68 cm

The adult can be identified by its small size, *bare yellow face*, red eyes, narrow bill and *elongated nape feathers*. In flight it shows a unique, *white diamond-shaped tail* and, from above, a *distinctive black line between the white upperwing coverts and the predominantly white upper secondaries*. The upperwing has a dark trailing edge, and the primaries are white on the upper surface. The immature has all-dark upperparts which are sometimes broadly tipped with white; it has a dark tail and is distinguished in flight from the immature Bearded Vulture (*see* page 12) by its smaller size and narrower head, bill and neck. It differs from the immature Hooded Vulture (*see* page 16) by having long nape feathers, a feathered throat, pale-tipped upperparts, and can be distinguished in flight by the shape of its tail, narrower wings, and underwing coverts which are paler than its flight feathers. It can also be distinguished from the similar immature Gymnogene (*see* page 88) by its shorter legs and lack of barring in the wings and tail. This vulture inhabits open, fairly dry country and is relatively common in east Africa. Once widespread, it is now an extremely rare vagrant in southern Africa, and is most frequently recorded there in the Etosha National Park in Namibia, with the only known breeding pair in southern Africa occurring in the Kaokoveld. It feeds mainly on carrion and other waste, and smashes Ostrich eggs with stones to feed on them. In east Africa it also scavenges around human settlements. It nests on cliffs and in east Africa it breeds from February until July.

Adult

Immature

Adult   *Sub-adult*   *Immature*

Adult

Immature

15

Hooded Vulture *Necrosyrtes monachus* (121) L 70 cm

The adult Hooded Vulture has a bare pink face and throat, a narrow bill, and a *pale crew-cut nape*. It has *silvery flight feathers* which contrast with the plain, dark underwing coverts, and less distinct white leggings than the Lappet-faced (*see* page 20) and White-headed (*see* page 18) vultures; it also lacks the white on the wings (and belly in the case of the White-headed Vulture) found in these two larger species. The immature vulture has a darker face, throat and nape, and lacks white leggings. It lacks the white line between the underwing coverts and flight feathers found on the under wing of the immature White-headed Vulture. In flight this vulture can be distinguished from Lappet-faced and White-headed vultures by its smaller size, and narrower head and bill. The Hooded Vulture is a resident species and is restricted to tall, well-developed woodland in southern Africa but is also found in more open country in east Africa. Gathering in small numbers around carcasses, these birds scavenge on small scraps left by larger vultures and in east Africa they can also be seen scavenging around human settlements, especially in Uganda. The Hooded Vulture was once more widespread in southern Africa, but is now only common there in protected areas such as the Kruger National Park in South Africa. It breeds from May until August in southern Africa and from January until July in east Africa. Its nests are usually well concealed within the canopies of tall trees.

Adult   *Immature*

NIGEL DENNIS

Adult

Immature

17

White-headed Vulture *Trigonoceps occipitalis* (125) L 85 cm

This medium-sized vulture is attractively patterne. The *head is a distinctive square shape*, and the bir has an *orange bill (blue at the base), ghostly whi down on the crown and nape*, and a pink face. Th dark chest contrasts with the white belly, and th leggings are white. The female has white second aries, while those of the male are dark. This differ ence is noticeable both at rest and in flight. Th immature is darker than the adult, having blac down on its crown and nape, and a dark belly. In flight both adults ar immatures show a *white line between the underwing coverts and th flight feathers*. This uncommon resident occurs in woodland where it often the first vulture to gather in small numbers around carcasses. may kill its own prey occasionally, but this remains unconfirmed. I southern Africa, it was once more widespread in woodland but is no rare except in protected areas such as the Kruger National Park. Breed ing occurs from May until August in southern Africa and throughout th year in east Africa. Nests are built in the canopies of tall trees.

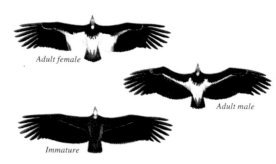

Adult female

Adult male

Immature

KEITH BEGG

Adult female

Adult male

Immature

19

Lappet-faced Vulture *Torgos tracheliotus* (124) L 115 cm

The imposing size, *bulky, naked wrinkled head and neck, massive yellow bill, and streaked underparts* are conspicuous features of this magnificent vulture. In flight its large size, solid head and neck, broad square wings, *white line through the centre of the underwing coverts*, and *white leggings* are distinctive. The immature has a dark bill and leggings, striking white dappling on its mantle, and in flight shows dark underparts. It differs from the much smaller immature Hooded Vulture (*see* page 16) in size, as well as in head and neck shape. It also lacks the white line between the underwing coverts and flight feathers characteristic of the immature White-headed Vulture (*see* page 18). This resident vulture frequents woodland and arid scrub, and in southern Africa it is uncommon outside of protected areas, although some individuals wander widely. It is the commonest vulture in the Namib Desert in Namibia. The Lappet-faced Vulture dominates other vultures at carcasses, and may kill its own prey occasionally but this remains unconfirmed. Breeding occurs from April until August in southern Africa and from February until July in east Africa when huge nests are built in the canopies of trees.

Adult

Immature

ANUP SHAH (ABPL)

Adult

20

Adults

Immature

21

African White-backed Vulture *Gyps africanus* (123) L 94 cm

This common vulture overlaps in many region with the Cape (*see* page 24) and Rüppell's (*se* page 26) vultures but usually outnumbers eithe at least in woodland areas. Compared to these tw species, it is *smaller*, has a *shorter neck* and a *les heavy bill*. The skin of the head, neck and two bar patches on the upper chest is black and the eyes ar dark. The adult shows a pure *white back* in flight The immature is darker than the adult and is heav ily streaked. Seen in flight, it shows a *white line through the centre of i underwing coverts*. A resident species, the White-backed Vulture i widespread in woodland but now rare in many such areas in souther Africa. It gathers in large numbers at carcasses. Breeding occurs in loos colonies and it nests in the canopies of tall trees from April until June i southern Africa and throughout the year in east Africa.

Adult

Immature

Adult

Sub-adult

Immature

Adult

Adult

Immature

23

Cape Vulture *Gyps coprotheres* (122) L 110 cm

This vulture can be *confused with the African White-backed Vulture* (*see* page 22) especially in the northern parts of southern Africa where both are frequently found at carcasses. The adult Cape Vulture, however, is *larger, has pale eyes, blue skin on the head, neck and two bare upper-chest patches, and a longer neck. The black spots seen on the otherwise pale last rows of upper- and underwing coverts* are useful in identification both when the birds are perched and in flight. The immature has dark eyes, *red skin on its head, neck and chest patches*, and faint underwing spots. *A thin white line along the last row of upperwing coverts* is visible in flight; it also *lacks the line through the centre of the underwing coverts* characteristic of the immature White-backed Vulture. The Cape Vulture shows *squarer wings and paler flight feathers* than the White-backed Vulture. Endemic to southern Africa, it is considered a threatened species, having lost large parts of its range. It is commonly found in the grasslands of the Eastern Cape, Lesotho and western KwaZulu-Natal, and also in the woodlands of northern South Africa, eastern Botswana, southern Zimbabwe and southwestern Mozambique, with isolated colonies occurring in the Western Cape (De Hoop Nature Reserve) and the north-central part of Namibia (Waterberg National Park). Cape Vultures breed from April until July and nest in colonies on tall cliffs.

Adult

Adult

Immature

Adult

Immature

CHRIS VAN ROOYEN

P.C. BENSON

25

Rüppell's Vulture *Gyps rueppellii* L 101 cm

This vulture can sometimes be *confused with the African White-backed Vulture (see* page 22) *in east Africa where both are frequently found at carcasses. It is larger, has a longer neck and a heavier bill.* The adult has a distinctive *yellow bill, pale eyes, and* grey or *red skin on its head,* neck and two bare patches on the upper chest. The upperparts are dark and speckled, creating the impression of a *strikingly mottled* bird. The *underparts and the underwing coverts are dark with lighter scaling,* and one bold line (front of the wing), and two or three indistinct, white lines run through the underwing coverts. The leggings and, especially, the powderpuff-like feathers around the base of the neck are white, often contrasting markedly with the rest of the plumage. The immature has a dark bill and eyes, with red skin on its head, neck and chest patches. This vulture is common in open, fairly dry country in east Africa. It has recently been recorded for the first time in the Northern Province of South Africa and in southern Zimbabwe, where it consorts with Cape Vultures on cliffs and around carcasses. The adult Rüppell's Vulture is distinctly different from the Cape Vulture *(see* page 24). The immature vulture closely resembles that species but is darker and more speckled. Rüppell's Vultures nest mainly from June until August in Kenya and at any time of the year in Tanzania. Breeding usually occurs in large colonies on tall cliffs.

Adult

Adult

26

Adult

Immature

27

Osprey *Pandion haliaetus* (170) L 55-58 cm

The adult and immature are similar in appearance, showing a *shaggy cream-coloured crown* with dark streaks, a *dark line through the eyes*, brown upperparts, a variable collar of streaks on the upper chest, and white underparts. The flight action, on long, bent wings, is relaxed but powerful. In flight a *black carpal patch*, black last row of underwing coverts, and faintly barred flight feathers and tail are visible. It differs from the immature African Fish Eagle (*see* page 58) by having a smaller and more protruding head, a dark line through the eyes, a slimmer build, narrower wings, a longer tail without a broad black tip, and barring in the wings and tail. The Osprey hunts in flight rather than from a perch. It feeds by diving deep into water, often almost completely submerging, to catch fish. It is an uncommon, non-breeding summer migrant but is a regular sight at large open water bodies, such as the Rift Valley lakes of east and central Africa, and especially along the coast, for example at Langebaan Lagoon in the Western Cape province of South Africa. Vagrants can occur at virtually any small wetland in Africa. Many immatures do not migrate north during winter, preferring to spend the winter in Africa.

BRENDAN RYAN (ABPL)

Brown Snake Eagle *Circaetus cinereus* (142) L 71-76 cm

This eagle has a large head, big yellow eyes, bare legs and a distinctive upright stance when perched. The adults are uniformly dark brown whereas the immatures have slightly mottled underparts. In flight the *distinctly pointed wings, dark brown underwing coverts* contrasting strongly with the *pale, silvery, unbarred flight feathers*, and barred tail are visible. The immature Brown Snake Eagle *resembles the immature Black-breasted Snake Eagle (see* page 30) but has a different wing shape, *darker less rufous brown colouring*, a more clearly barred tail, and lacks bars in the flight feathers. The Brown Snake Eagle inhabits woodlands but vagrants often wander widely. Snakes, their main prey, are hunted from tall exposed perches; unlike the Black-breasted Snake Eagle it does not hunt in flight. Although many individuals are present throughout the year in southern Africa, it appears largely to be a non-breeding summer migrant. During summer this eagle is occasionally recorded in the Western and Eastern Cape provinces, well south of the known breeding range. The Brown Snake Eagle breeds mainly from July until March in southern Africa and from February until May in central and east Africa.

Adult

PETER PICKFORD (SIL)

Adult

29

Black-breasted Snake Eagle *Circaetus gallicus* (143) L 63-68 cm

The adult eagle is a medium-sized raptor with a large head, yellow eyes, black upperparts and chest, plain white underparts, a barred tail, and bare legs. The wings are long, square and white below with barred flight feathers. The immature has brown upperparts, rufous underparts and underwing coverts, and a pale, indistinctly barred tail and flight feathers. The adult *resembles the adult Martial Eagle (see page 34)* but is smaller, and lacks a crest and spots on the underparts; in flight it can be distinguished by *white underwing coverts* and flight feathers, and *conspicuous bars on the wings and tail*. The immature differs from the Brown Snake Eagle (*see* page 29) by having a different wing shape, a *paler more rufous colour*, barred flight feathers, and a paler, less clearly barred tail. Black-breasted Snake Eagles inhabit woodland and open habitats such as Karoo and dry grassland. Non-breeding birds sometimes form communal roosts in grassland areas; for example around Johannesburg. This eagle usually hunts its prey (snakes and lizards) while soaring and it hovers frequently. It breeds from March until October in southern Africa and from November until May in east Africa in small nests in the canopies of trees. There are three subspecies of this eagle and each may constitute a separate species. The Black-breasted Snake Eagle *C.g. pectoralis* is widespread, occurring virtually throughout the region. Beaudouin's Snake Eagle *C.g. beaudouini* occurs in northern Uganda (where it replaces the Black-breasted Snake Eagle) and northwestern Kenya. The Short-toed Snake Eagle *C.g. gallicus* is a rare non-breeding vagrant to northern Kenya and Uganda during the northern winter. Beaudouin's Snake Eagle and the Short-toed Snake Eagle differ from the Black-breasted Snake Eagle by being paler above and on the chest, and barred on the belly. The Short-toed Snake Eagle resembles Beaudouin's Snake Eagle but is paler in colour and less distinctly barred in the wings and tail. Unlike the Black-breasted Snake Eagle, the immatures of the Beaudouin's Snake Eagle and the Short-toed Snake Eagle resemble the adults.

Adult

Sub-adult

Immature

NICO MYBURGH

Adult with chick

KOOS DELPORT (PHOTO ACCESS)

Immature

31

Southern Banded Snake Eagle *Circaetus fasciolatus* (144) L 55-60 cm

In flight this small eagle resembles a large goshawk. The head, upperparts and upper chest are grey-brown, the lower chest and belly are barred and the legs are bare. In flight it shows short rounded wings, barred underwing coverts and flight feathers, a broad black band on the trailing edge of the wing, and a long tail. The uppertail shows three dark bands, and the undertail three dark bands and a fourth broad dark band at the tip. This bird can be *distinguished from the Western Banded Snake Eagle* (*see* page 33) by its *longer tail with different patterning and more extensive barring on the underparts and underwing*. However, the two species are unlikely to be confused since they do not overlap in distribution. The immature Southern Banded Snake Eagle is browner above than the adult, with a streaked upper chest, and paler underparts. It *resembles the immature Western Banded Snake Eagle* but has a *different tail pattern*. Although unobtrusive, this rare and near-threatened species often calls loudly in the morning. It inhabits coastal forest, close to water. In southern Africa it can be seen in the coastal nature reserves of northeastern KwaZulu-Natal. Breeding occurs from July until October.

Adult

PETER PICKFORD (SIL)

Adult

This small bird of prey has a large head and unfeathered legs. Its plumage is plain grey-brown, usually with some barring on the lower belly. In flight it shows short rounded wings, and barred flight feathers; the outer and leading edge of the underwing coverts, however, are unbarred. A broad black band is visible on the trailing edge of the wing, and the tail is dark with one broad white bar. The Western Banded Snake Eagle *resembles the Southern Banded Snake Eagle (see page 32), but has a shorter tail with different barring, and less barring on the underparts and underwing.* The distributions of the two species do not overlap. The immature bird is browner above than the adult with a streaked upper chest, and paler underparts. It *resembles the immature Southern Banded Snake Eagle but has a different tail pattern.* The Western Banded Snake Eagle is restricted to tall riverine woodland. In the southern African region, it is usually best observed in the Chobe National Park in Botswana. It builds well-concealed nests in tall trees from December until April, and can be highly vocal during the breeding season. The Western Banded Snake Eagle preys mainly on snakes.

Adult

DAVE RICHARDS

Adult

Martial Eagle *Polemaetus bellicosus* (140) L 78-83 cm

The Martial Eagle is Africa's largest and most imposing eagle. It has a slight crest and feathered legs. The adult has black upperparts, a black head and chest, *white underparts with small dark spots* and all-dark underwings. The immature can be identified by its white underparts and underwing coverts, and pale grey upperparts. The adult can be *distinguished from the adult Black-breasted Snake Eagle (see page 30)* by its larger size, crest and spotted lower underparts, and in flight *by its dark underwing coverts and lack of conspicuous bars on the tail and dark flight feathers*. The immature Martial Eagle can be separated from some of the similar vultures in flight by a different head and neck shape. It can be distinguished from the immature Crowned Eagle (*see* page 36) by its shape (relatively long wings and a short tail), the absence of faint rufous on the underparts, and the presence of grey on the sides of the upper chest; it also lacks conspicuous bars in the flight feathers and tail, and has unmarked leggings. This eagle occurs in all habitats but is scarce outside of protected and uninhabited areas. It preys on a wide variety of animals, including medium-sized mammals, large birds and monitor lizards. It breeds from February until November and builds huge nests in trees or on pylons.

Adult

Immature

Adult

Immature

Immature

34

Adult

35

Crowned Eagle *Stephanoaetus coronatus* (141) L 80-90 cm

This large raptor is Africa's most powerful eagle. It has a pronounced crest and feathered legs. The adult's upperparts are dark and its *underparts heavily patterned with black, white and rufous*. In flight it shows *short, broad wings, rufous under-wing coverts, heavily barred flight feathers, and long barred tail*. The immature is pale grey above and white below. It can be *distinguished from the immature Martial Eagle (see page 34) by its shape* (relatively short wings and long tail), *lack of grey on the sides of the upper chest*, and presence of rufous on the underparts; it has *conspicuous barring in the flight feathers and tail*, and *spotted leggings*. This eagle is restricted to forests, including plantations of alien trees close to natural forest, and it also inhabits tall, dense woodland, especially in the north of its range. It is a fierce predator and preys largely on medium-sized mammals such as monkeys, hyrax and small antelope. It has distinctive pendulous, aerial display flight, which is accompanied by far-carrying, rhythmical chanting call. It builds a huge nest in tall forest trees, and lays its eggs from June until November in southern Africa and throughout the year in east Africa. Each breeding attempt can take over a year from egg-laying until the final independence of the chick.

Immature

Adult

Immature

Immature

Immature

NICO MYBURGH

Adult

Black Eagle *Aquila verreauxii* (131) L 84 cm

This large eagle has an all-black plumage with a *white cross on the back*, and a conspicuous yellow cere and feet. It has a small head, a long neck, broad shoulders, and long feathered legs. The shape of the wings in flight is unique, the *outer wing being very broad*, and the *inner wing markedly narrower*, and there is an obvious pale wing panel in the primaries. The immature can be identified by its *blond crown*, black face and front of the neck, *rufous mantle*, and conspicuous, pale *V-shaped markings on the underparts*; it has a pale bill, pale shoulder patches and black smudges on the grey leggings. A consummate flier, this eagle is rarely seen flapping, relying on thermals and the wind shear associated with broken country to stay aloft. It is a relatively common resident but is restricted to mountainous regions. It feeds mainly on hyrax, but also on other medium-sized mammals, tortoises, large birds and carrion. It usually hunts on the wing, sometimes in pairs. It breeds from February until August and lays its eggs in large nests on cliffs, and occasionally in trees.

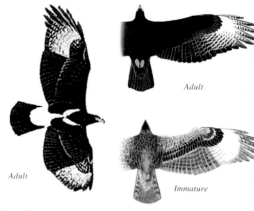

Adult

Adult

Immature

Immature

ALBERT FRONEMAN

Adult

ALBERT FRONEMAN

Immature

39

Wahlberg's Eagle *Aquila wahlbergi* (135) L 55-60 cm

This small eagle has a *slight crest*, brown eyes and feathered legs. The plumage colour is highly variable, from light to dark brown with a mixture of light and dark plumage in some individuals. Immatures resemble the adults. In flight it shows *square shaped wings, and a long square tail that is usually held closed.* During the typically leisurely soaring flight, the head is held facing downwards. The underwing coverts are darker than the flight feathers. A scarce light form occurs which is virtually pure white on the head, neck, underparts and underwing coverts. This eagle is a breeding summer migrant to southern and east Africa, arriving in late August and departing by early April to spend the winter north of the equator. Some birds are resident on the equator. It is the commonest of the woodland breeding eagles, and occurs in most woodland types. Hunting on the wing, it preys mainly on reptiles, small to medium-sized birds and small mammals. Wahlberg's Eagles breed from August until November. They are possibly more closely related to the 'hawk eagles' of the genus *Hieraaetus* than to the true *Aquila* eagles.

Dark form

Pale form

Dark form

Buff form

Dark form

Pale and dark forms

Booted Eagle *Hieraaetus pennatus* (136) L 48-52 cm

This diminutive eagle has feathered legs, and occurs in two colour forms, a common pale form with cream-coloured underparts and underwing coverts, and a rarer dark form which is plain brown. Some individuals show rufous underparts. The pale form shows lightly streaked underparts, dark spots on the pale underwing coverts, and a head that appears hooded. Seen in flight, all colour forms show a *pale V-shape across the upperwing and back*, similar to that found in the Yellow-billed Kite. This eagle also has a *distinctive white spot where the leading edge of the wing joins the body*, a narrow white rump, and a *pale tail*. Immatures are similar to adults. One population breeds in western South Africa and Namibia, and disperses throughout southern and central Africa when not breeding. Another population comprises non-breeding summer migrants to southern, central and east Africa from Europe and Asia. Booted Eagles occur in a wide range of habitats and are most commonly found where fynbos meets the Karoo in southwestern South Africa. It is usually seen soaring and it perches mainly on cliff faces. It preys on small to medium-sized birds, small mammals, reptiles and insects. Breeding occurs during September when well-concealed nests are built on low cliffs.

Pale form

Dark form

Dark form

Pale form

Pale form

Dark form

Tawny Eagle *Aquila rapax* (132) L 65-72 cm

This medium-sized eagle has a distinctive rounded head, oval nostrils, plumage which appears ragged and fully feathered legs. In flight the wing shows an S-shaped trailing edge. The bird's colouring is highly variable: either plain rufous, blond or light brown (adult males and immatures) or dark brown and streaked (adult females), but *always with some tawny colouring in the plumage*. This species *resembles the Steppe Eagle (see page 46) but differs by having a generally paler plumage or streaks, pale yellow eyes (in the adult), a gape that extends only to the centre of the eye, and by lacking a ginger nape patch*. The immature has indistinct white lines on the under- and upperwing coverts, along the trailing edge of the wing, and on the tip of the tail; it lacks the obvious white rump of the immature Steppe Eagle. This common resident inhabits all woodland types including lightly wooded areas but is scarce outside of protected areas especially in southern Africa. It preys on a wide variety of small animals, feeds on carrion and pirates from large birds. This eagle breeds from March until October and its nests are built in the canopies of trees.

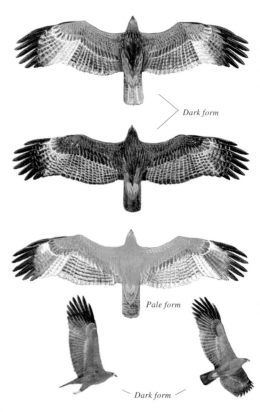

Dark form

Pale form

Dark form

Pale form

Dark form

45

Steppe Eagle *Aquila nipalensis* (133) L 75 cm

This eagle resembles the Tawny Eagle (*see* page 44) but is *plainer, darker brown* and *lacks tawny colouring in the plumage*. The elongated *gape extends beyond the centre of the dark eyes*. The adult has oval nostrils, a ginger nape patch, and feathered legs. Seen in flight from above, it shows a pale patch at the base of the inner primaries. The immature shows a broad white line on the underwing and upperwing coverts, along the trailing edge of the wing, and on the tip of the tail. Viewed in flight from above, an obvious white rump and a white patch in the primaries are visible. Two subspecies occur in southern Africa: the race *A.n. orientalis* is smaller and paler, with a less pronounced gape than *A.n. nipalensis*, and is difficult to distinguish from the Tawny Eagle. The Steppe Eagle is a non-breeding summer migrant to woodland areas. It often perches on the ground, and is attracted to termite emergences and quelea breeding colonies. It can occur in large flocks with Tawny and Lesser Spotted eagles. This species is considered by some to be a subspecies of the Tawny Eagle.

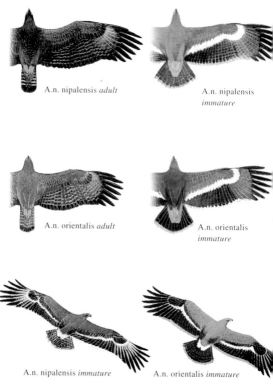

A.n. nipalensis *adult*

A.n. nipalensis
immature

A.n. orientalis *adult*

A.n. orientalis
immature

A.n. nipalensis *immature*

A.n. orientalis *immature*

PETER PICKFORD (SIL)

Adult

PETER STEYN

Immature

47

Lesser Spotted Eagle *Aquila pomarina* (134) L 57-64 cm

'Stove-pipe' feathered leggings are a characteristic feature of the Lesser Spotted Eagle. In flight the tail appears fairly short, and the *wings long and slightly drooping* with pale under- and upperwing coverts and contrasting darker flight feathers. The adult is plain dark brown with a small head, pale yellow eyes, and *round nostrils*. Seen in flight from above, it shows a very narrow white rump and a slight white patch at the base of the primaries. The immature can be identified by its brown eyes, ginger nape patch and lightly streaked underparts. It has *two rows of white spots on the upper wing coverts*, indistinct white tips to the underwing coverts, flight feathers and tail, a narrow white rump, and a small white patch on the upper primaries. This eagle resembles the Tawny (*see* page 44) and Steppe eagles (*see* page 46) but lacks barring in the primaries and tail. It can be distinguished from Wahlberg's Eagle (*see* page 40) by the shape of its head, wings and tail, by the white colouring in its plumage and by the adult's yellow, not brown eyes. The immature birds can be distinguished from the adult and immature Wahlberg's Eagles by their ginger nape patch. This species is a scarce, non-breeding summer migrant to woodland areas in southern and central Africa. It is usually only present in east Africa while on migration between its European breeding grounds and its southern and central African wintering quarters. This eagle is attracted to termite emergences and quelea breeding colonies.

Adult

Immature

Adult

CLEM HAAGNER (ABPL)

48

eater Spotted Eagle *Aquila clanga* L 60-70 cm

The adult of this medium-sized eagle is uniformly dark brown to blackish in colour, with a *purple sheen* to the upperparts. It resembles the adult Lesser Spotted Eagle (*see* page 48) but has brown eyes and is slightly bigger, darker in colour and broader winged. Like that species it also has *stove-pipe leggings* and *round nostrils*. In flight it differs from the Lesser Spotted Eagle by showing *blackish-brown wing coverts that in some cases e darker than the flight feathers*. It resembles the Steppe Eagle (*see* ge 46) but lacks barring in the outer primaries and tail. The immature s a white rump, a barred tail, and distinctive *bold spots on its shoul-rs, back and upperwing coverts*. These spots are often larger and more merous than those found in the immature Lesser Spotted Eagle; the mature Greater Spotted Eagle also lacks the ginger nape patch char-teristic of that species. A rare pale form of the Greater Spotted Eagle curs. This globally threatened eagle is a rare vagrant to east Africa om October until April. Most records of sightings come from the Rift alley region. Its prey is varied and it is attracted to locust swarms and rmite emergences. It is occasionally found in small flocks and some-nes consorts with Steppe Eagles among which it is easily overlooked.

Adult

H. & J. ERIKSEN

Immature

Immature

W.S. CLARK

49

Eastern Imperial Eagle *Aquila heliaca* L 72-84 cm

This eagle has a *large and heavy build, a powe[r]ful beak and contrasting plumage*. In flight wings and neck appear long. The adult has pa[le] brown eyes, and a *pale crown and nape* whi[ch] contrasts with the rest of the dark brown pluma[ge]. The *head and neck feathers are long and shag[gy]* and there is a small *white patch on the mant[le]*. The flight feathers are blackish and paler than t[he] wing coverts. The greyish tail has a broad bla[ck] band above the whitish tip and contrasts with the pale vent. The *imma[-]ture* is pale or dark brown and is *streaked or mottled* in appearan[ce] above and below. The inner primaries of the immature are pale brow[n] and contrast with the remaining darker flight feathers. The upperwi[ng] coverts show pale narrow bars, similar to those found on the upperwi[ng] of the immature Steppe Eagle (*see* page 46) but unlike that speci[es] there is *no pale line in the underwing*. The immature has brown eyes, white rump, and a plain brown tail with a white tip. Like the immatu[re] Eastern Imperial Eagle, adult Tawny Eagles (*see* page 44) can al[so] appear streaked, but they are smaller and lack bars in the upperwi[ng] coverts. The Eastern Imperial Eagle is globally threatened and is a ra[re] migrant to grasslands in east Africa from November until March. It [is] easily overlooked amongst other large brown eagles, especially Stepp[e] Eagles. It feeds mainly on small to medium-sized mammals and carrio[n].

Immature

Immature

The upright stance, *long crest* and black plumage render this unusual eagle unmistakable. The feathers on its legs can be either white (males and immatures) or dark brown (females). It flies with rapid, shallow wing-beats and shows a white wing panel in the primaries during flight. When soaring, the Long-crested Eagle appears similar to the Black Eagle (*see* page 38) but is much smaller, has a *barred tail* and a different wing shape.

lowever, these two birds are unlikely to be confused since they do not hare the same habitat. The immature eagle resembles the adult but has shorter crest and grey eyes; the adult's eyes are yellow. This fairly ommon resident inhabits well-developed woodland, including planta-ons of alien trees. It is usually found at the edge of marshy areas where it often hunts rodents from tall perches. Non-breeding vagrants vander widely outside the usual range. This species' ability to exploit orestry plantations has enabled it to expand into previously treeless rassland regions in some places. In other areas, however, its numbers ave decreased due to the degradation of wetlands. The nests of these irds are well concealed in tall trees, including alien trees. Breeding an occur at any time of the year throughout the region.

PETER PICKFORD (SIL)

African Hawk Eagle *Hieraaetus spilogaster* (137) L 60-65 cm

This medium-sized eagle has a black head and upperparts, *white underparts with heavy black streaking*, and feathered legs. In flight from below, it shows distinctive broad, rounded outer wings and narrow inner wings reminiscent of the Black Eagle (see page 38). Although mainly white below, it shows black streaks on the under wing coverts and a *dark trailing edge to the wing* (formed by the broad black tips to the flight feathers); a *pale wing panel* can be discerned in the primaries. The faintly barred *tail has a broad black tip*. The *immature is dark rufous below* with streaked underparts and a *faintly barred tail* and flight feathers. Although common in woodland, this eagle is inconspicuous and rarely soars. It is usually seen in pairs and preys mainly on large birds, and small to medium-sized mammals. It breeds from April until November and lays its eggs in large nests in trees, and in east Africa also occasionally on cliffs. This species is considered by some to be a sub-species of the Eurasian Bonelli's Eagle, *H. fasciatus*.

Adult

Immature

Adult

Immature

52

LORNA STANTON (ABPL)

Adult

JOHN CARLYON

Immature

53

Ayres' Eagle *Hieraaetus ayresii* (138) L 46-55 cm

This small dashing eagle has feathered legs and a slight crest. The adult's upperparts are black but the rest of the plumage varies. It usually has a black hood on the head but occasionally the head is markedly white. The *underparts are generally white spotted with black* although they may be all black. In flight it shows spotted underwing coverts, *black bars on the flight feathers and tail* and a white spot where the leading edge of the wing joins the body. The *immature is pale rufous* with faint streaking on the underparts, and has a *barred tail* and flight feathers. Adults and immatures differ from the African Hawk Eagle (*see page 52*) by being smaller and more compact, having a different wing shape and a crest, clearer barring in the wings and tail, and they lack a wing panel in the primaries. Also, the adult has a more heavily marked appearance, usually a white forehead, spotting (not streaking) on the underparts and underwing coverts, and a white spot on the leading edge of the wing. Immatures have yellow (not brown) eyes, are paler rufous on the underparts, have distinctive buff tips to the feathers, and less distinct streaking on the underparts. This species is unaccountably rare throughout its range. It is a non-breeding summer migrant to a wide variety of habitats in northeastern South Africa and eastern Botswana but is largely sedentary elsewhere. Breeding occurs from March until September and nests are built in tall woodland. Ayres' Eagles prey mainly on medium-sized birds, and often frequent towns.

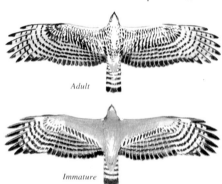

Adult

Immature

R.R. HARTLEY

Immature

Adult dark form

Adult pale form

Bateleur Eagle *Terathopius ecaudatus* (146) L 55-70 cm

This eagle is unmistakable with its large head, *bare red face, black, chestnut and grey plumage,* stocky body, *red legs* and short tail. In flight it shows *pointed wings,* white underwing coverts and *legs extended beyond the tail.* The male's flight feathers are black and the female's are white with a black trailing edge. This difference is also noticeable in the folded wing when perched. A rare form has a cream-coloured back. The Bateleur Eagle can be confused with the Jackal Buzzard (*see page 80*) in flight but lacks the white and rufous on the underparts, and the black underwing coverts of that species; these two birds also do not share the same habitat. The immature is brown with blue-green facial skin, and in flight its legs usually do not extend beyond the tail. The Bateleur Eagle has a distinctive *low, fast, direct and tilting flight action,* with upswept wings. It inhabits woodland plains but has become extinct in much of its former range in southern Africa due to poisoning. A highly conspicuous eagle, it spends most of the day in flight at a low altitude. It hunts by descending in a tight spiral on birds and small mammals. Adults also feed on small carrion, and immatures are attracted to large carcasses. This species breeds mainly from December until March and builds well-concealed nests in trees.

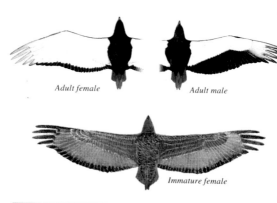

Adult female   *Adult male*

Immature female

CLEM HAAGNER (ABPL)

Immature

Adult male (left) and female (right)

Immature

57

African Fish Eagle *Haliaeetus vocifer* (148) L 63-73 cm

This eagle is regarded by many as Africa's most familiar bird of prey. The adult has a distinctive *white head and chest*, chestnut shoulders and belly, a white tail, and bare legs. In flight the white head, *broad wings with chestnut underwing coverts*, and short white tail are visible. The immature's untidy plumage may vary in colour and pattern; the background colour of the underparts is initially rufous, but later turns whitish and the underparts always have dark streaks and spots; the white *tail has a broad black tip*. The immature can be confused with the Osprey (*see* page 28) but is larger, broader winged, more marked below, lacks barring in the flight feathers and tail, and has a black tail tip. It also lacks the dark line through the eye characteristic of the Osprey. Unlike Ospreys, African Fish Eagles hunt from a perch, rather than in flight. This eagle is associated with larger wetlands and rivers throughout sub-Saharan Africa, where it feeds primarily on fish. In southern Africa it occurs most commonly in the Okavango Swamps of Botswana. The major floodplains and Rift Valley lakes of central and east Africa are also strongholds of this eagle. Although the African Fish Eagle has suffered from wetland degradation in some areas, it has benefited from the construction of large dams, especially in southern Africa. This species has a characteristic far-carrying call. It breeds from March until October and nests in trees, sometimes on cliffs, but always close to water.

Adult

Immature

Adult

Adult

Immature

59

Common Black-shouldered Kite *Elanus caeruleus* (127) L 30 cm

This small, ubiquitous kite, one of Africa's most familiar birds of prey, is highly distinctive in appearance. It has a relatively large head, a stocky body, long pointed wings, a short tail, and short thick legs and talons. The head is white, the eyes are bright red, the upperparts blue-grey with *black shoulder patches*, and the underparts are white. In flight the wings are characteristically bent and held in a fairly high V-shape when soaring. Seen from below, it shows white underwing coverts and secondaries, and a white tail. Immature Black-shouldered Kites resemble adults but have brown, yellow or orange eyes, pale buff-tipped upperparts, and indistinct rust-coloured markings on the underparts. Although widespread, the Black-shouldered Kite is particularly attracted to agricultural areas and avoids densely wooded and arid regions. It typically perches along roadsides, often wagging its tail, or hovers in the air while hunting rodents. It is most active at dawn and dusk. This species often roosts communally, and lays its eggs at any time of year in flimsy, well-concealed nests in the canopies of trees.

Adult

GERALD HOBERMAN

Adult

60

This elegant raptor *resembles the Common Black-shouldered Kite (see page 60)* but is *slimmer, lacks the black shoulder patch* of that species and has a *long, deeply forked tail.* It is usually seen in flight and shows a *thick black line across the leading edge of the outer underwing coverts.* Its flight is buoyant and tern-like. The immature bird has buff tips to the feathers of the upperparts and its tail is not as deeply forked as that of the adult.

This kite inhabits dry open country in east Africa and usually occurs in flocks. It is migratory, being a breeding visitor to northwestern Kenya from March until October and a non-breeding visitor to the Kenyan coast from November until March. A small resident breeding population is found in the Kedong Valley in southeastern Kenya. This species' main prey comprises insects which are hunted while soaring or hovering but it also takes lizards and rodents during the breeding season. It is attracted to grass fires and locust swarms. Like the Common Black-shouldered Kite, it occasionally wags its tail up and down when perched. The African Swallow-tailed Kite frequently roosts communally and breeds in loose colonies, building small nests in thorn bushes, usually from March until June.

Adult

DAVE RICHARDS

Black Kite *Milvus migrans* (126) L 55 cm

This kite's leisurely flight action is distinctive, o[n] long bent wings, its *triangular tail twisted fro[m] side to side* and its head hanging. A *pal[e] V-shaped marking* across the back and upper wings is visible in flight. At rest, the closed *tail [is] deeply forked and appears noticeably indented i[n]* flight. Two subspecies of this kite are common i[n] the region and they may represent separat[e] species. The Yellow-billed Kite *M.m. parasitu[s]* breeds in Africa. It is largely a migrant to central and east Africa fro[m] August until March, and virtually exclusively a migrant to souther[n] Africa during the same period (summer). The Black Kite *M.m. migran[s]* is a non-breeding summer migrant from Eurasia. Both subspecies ar[e] common to abundant in the region avoiding only arid areas but th[e] Black Kite is less common in southern Africa and does not occur i[n] the southernmost parts of South Africa. The adult Yellow-billed Kit[e] differs from the adult Black Kite in having a diagnostic *yellow bill* an[d] plain brown plumage on the head and body. The adult Black Kite has [a] *black bill* and a *pale, almost whitish, head*. The tail of the Yellow[-] billed Kite is more deeply forked than that of the Black Kite. Th[e] immatures of the two subspecies are similar: both have black bills an[d] pale streaking on the body, although the streaking is less marked in th[e] immature Yellow-billed Kite. This highly conspicuous kite spend[s] most of the day on the wing, congregating around suitable food source[s] such as carrion, and also takes small live prey. It is attracted to ro[ad] kills and has a characteristic side-slipping flight action when descen[d]ing on food. The Yellow-billed Kite breeds from August unt[il] December in southern Africa and mainly from November until Mar[ch] in east Africa and lays its eggs in untidy nests in trees. It has [a] distinctive, tremulous, whinnying call.

M.m. migrans *adult*

M.m. parasitus *adult*   M.m. migrans *adult*   M.m. parasitus

M.m. migrans *adult*

DAVE RICHARDS

M.m. parasitus *adult (left) and immature (right)*

CHRIS VAN ROOYEN

63

African Marsh Harrier *Circus ranivorus* (165) L 44-49 cm

Like all harriers the African Marsh Harrier has a distinctive owl-like cowl of feathers around its face, and a long tail and legs. The adult is variably brown in colour, sometimes showing paler speckling, especially around the head and shoulders. It has a rufous belly and leggings, and a *barred tail and flight feathers*. The sexes are similar but the male is greyer and the female is usually more rufous on the underparts and darker on the upperparts. The immature is plainer and darker brown with a *pale band across the chest*, and often shows a poorly defined pale crown, throat and shoulders. The flight action is fairly buoyant, usually low down with the wings held in a high V-shape. The African Marsh Harrier is regularly seen at larger wetlands with marshy vegetation, but is becoming uncommon, especially in South Africa, due to wetland degradation. In flight it quarters repeatedly over marshy areas, hunting for rodents and small to medium-sized birds. This resident harrier nests on the ground in dense wetland vegetation from February until October.

Adult

Immature

Adult

Immature

Adult

Immature

European Marsh Harrier *Circus aeruginosus* (164) L 48-56 cm

The male is highly distinctive with its pale head and *unbarred grey tail*. The *flight feathers and last row of upperwing coverts are unbarred grey above*, and the flight feathers unbarred white below. There is a *dark trailing edge to the wing* and *conspicuous black tips to the primaries*. The rest of the plumage is brown, sometimes showing a pale rump. The .is dark brown with well defined, plain cream patches on the crown, throat and shoulders. It has *unbarred wings and tail*, and sometimes shows pale patch on the chest. The immature resembles the female but often lacks the cream-coloured plumage. The bird's flight action is fairly buoyant, usually low down with the wings held in a high V-shape. The adult male *resembles the African Marsh Harrier (see page 64)* habits, and the female and immature also resemble that species appearance, but *lack barring in the flight feathers and tail*. This non breeding summer migrant inhabits wetlands. It is common in east Africa and has been recorded with increasing frequency in the northeastern parts of southern Africa. It preys mainly on rodents and water birds.

Adult male

Adult male

Adult female

Immature

Adult male

Adult female

Immature

Adult male

Immature

Montagu's Harrier *Circus pygargus* (166) L 40-47 cm

At rest the male shows a grey head, chest and upperparts, white underparts with chestnut streaks, and a black line through the folded wing. In flight a broad black wedge is visible in the primaries of the outer wing, and the underwing coverts are streaked; one black line runs through the secondaries on the upperwing, while two lines are visible from below. The flight action is buoyant and the wings are held in a high V-shape. The females and immatures are *difficult to distinguish from the females and immatures of the Pallid Harrier* (*see* page 70). The female is brown and has streaked underparts and a narrow white rump. The key facial features that distinguish it from the female Pallid Harrier are the *narrow line at the rear of the eye* that hardly obscures the *white cheek*, and the *absence of a white collar* on the back of the neck. In flight from below *pale spaces* are visible *between the dark bands on the secondaries*; from above *barring across the secondaries* can be discerned. The immature resembles the female but has unmarked chestnut underparts. Adults have yellow eyes and immatures have dark eyes. A rare melanistic form resembles the Black Harrier (*see* page 72) but lacks the white rump of that species. This species is a non-breeding summer migrant to grasslands and open areas in woodland, and its numbers have decreased dramatically in recent decades. It is fairly common in east Africa, but is scarce in southern Africa. It feeds on insects, lizards and birds.

| *Adult male* | *Adult female* | *Immature* | *Adult male* |

Immature

Adult male

Adult female

69

Pallid Harrier *Circus macrourus* (167) L 40-48 cm

The male has light grey upperparts and pure white underparts. In flight a narrow wedge of black is visible in the primaries of the outer wing. The flight action is buoyant with wings held in a high V-shape. The female is brown above and has streaked underparts and a narrow white rump. Viewed in flight from below, *narrow, pale spaces* are visible between the dark bands *on the second aries*; from above *no barring can be discerned in the secondaries*. Females and immatures resemble the females and immatures of the Montagu's Harrier (*see* page 68). The key features that distinguish the female Pallid Harrier from the female Montagu's Harrier are the *broad line at the rear of the eye* obscuring the white cheek, and the *white collar* on the back of the neck. Immatures resemble females but have dark sides to the neck and unmarked chestnut underparts. Adults have yellow eyes and immatures have dark eyes. This species is a non-breeding summer migrant to grassland and woodland and is fairly common in east Africa but scarce in southern Africa. It feeds on insects and birds. Pallid Harriers are globally near-threatened.

Adult male *Adult female* *Immature* *Adult male*

Immature

Adult male

Immature

71

Black Harrier *Circus maurus* (168) L 48-53 cm

At rest, the adult is *all-black* in colour and shows an obvious facial disk. In flight a *broad white rump*, white flight feathers with a broad black trailing edge, and a black-and-white barred tail are visible. The flight action is buoyant with wings held in a high V-shape. The immature is dark grey with contrasting pale ash-grey colouration and is characterized by a dark head, dark mottling on the chest forming a *distinct gorget*, a pale ash-grey belly, and lightly streaked flanks. In flight its underwing coverts appear streaked with a line of heavy streaking along the rear edge; it has pale flight feathers with a broad dark trailing edge, barred secondaries and black-tipped primaries. Viewed from above, the immature shows distinctive *pale windows in the primaries*. The sexes are alike. Near-threatened and endemic to southern Africa, the Black Harrier inhabits fynbos, Karoo and grassland, and is locally common in the extreme southwest; it is usually a less common, non-breeding winter migrant elsewhere in its range. It is easily seen in lowland fynbos in larger nature reserves in this vegetation type, for example in the West Coast and Bontebok national parks and in De Hoop Nature Reserve in South Africa. Largely independent of wetlands, the Black Harrier nests and forages in open fynbos, Karoo, grassland and agricultural areas. It feeds mainly on small birds, rodents and insects. Nests are built on the ground in dense vegetation from July until September.

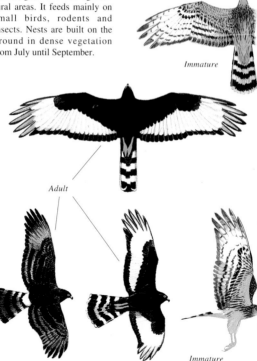

Immature

Adult

Immature

Adult

Immature

73

Forest Buzzard *Buteo oreophilus* (150) L 45 cm

The adult Forest Buzzard has brown eyes and white underparts with dark spots. The South African subspecies has an *extensive white band across the chest*. The tail is cinnamon-coloured with narrow bars and a broad dark tip. The adult resembles the adult Steppe Buzzard (*see* page 76) but is slightly smaller and has whiter *underparts without any barring*. In flight it shows shorter and broader wings, whiter underwing coverts and shorter tail than that species. The overall shape of the wing is similar to that of a miniature Jackal Buzzard (*see* page 80). The immature has pale yellow eyes, dark streaks on the white underparts, and lacks a broad dark tip to the tail. It is virtually *indistinguishable from the immature Steppe Buzzard* except for the streaks on the underparts which are *more tear-shaped*. The Forest Buzzard occurs in forests or plantations of alien trees close to natural forest. It is most common in South Africa in coastal forests between Cape Town and Port Elizabeth, especially in the Knysna Forest. It appears to be a winter migrant to the inland montane forests further north in South Africa. This noisy bird has a high-pitched barking call and feeds mainly on rodents. It breeds from March until October and lays its eggs in well-concealed nests in tall trees. The South African subspecies *B.o. trizonatus* may be a separate species from the subspecies *B.o. oreophilus*, the Mountain Buzzard found in east and central Africa.

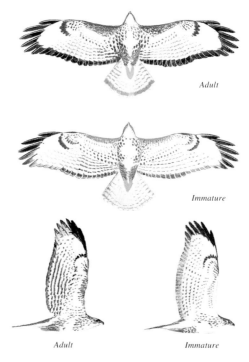

Adult

Immature

Adult   *Immature*

Adult

Immature

75

Steppe Buzzard *Buteo buteo vulpinus* (149) L 45-50 cm

The adult has brown eyes and a cinnamon coloured tail with narrow bars and a broad dark tip. The pattern on the underparts is variable. The upper chest is usually brown and separated from the *barred belly* by a broad mottled band on the lower chest. The underparts of some adults can also be either plain brown or broadly banded rufous. The immature has yellow eyes, white underparts with dark spots or streaks, and lacks the broad dark tip to the tail characteristic of the adult. This buzzard shows mottled brown underwing coverts in flight, paler flight feathers, a dark carpal patch, dark wing tips and trailing edge to the wing, and a cinnamon tail. It is a non-breeding summer migrant and is found in a wide variety of habitats, including forested areas and plantations but avoids arid areas. It is most common in the Western Cape province of South Africa. In east Africa, it is common during migration from September to November and from February to March. It frequently perches on roadside poles and preys on rodents. This species belongs to the northern Scandinavian and European Russian race of the Eurasian Buzzard.

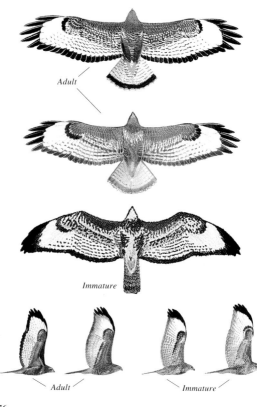

Adult

Immature

Adult   *Immature*

PETER PICKFORD (SIL)

Adult

CLEM HAAGNER (ABPL)

Immature

Long-legged Buzzard *Buteo rufinus* (151) L 51-66 cm

This buzzard is large and eagle-like and it plumage is highly variable. It usually has a *pal head*, often with a moustachial stripe, a brown o rufous body, and a *dark belly*. In flight the *wing appear long (especially the outer wing) an square*, showing a *pronounced high V-shape whe soaring*. From below it shows a *wide, dark carpa patch*, white flight feathers with black tips to th primaries, and a dark trailing edge to the win From above a slight pale wing panel is visible in the primaries. Th long, broad *tail is white* or pale rufous in colour. The dark form of th buzzard shows a broad dark tip to the tail. The immature is similar t the adult but its belly and carpal patches are not as dark as those of th adult, and it has a lightly barred tail. It is distinguished from the Stepp Buzzard (*see* page 76) and the immature Jackal Buzzard (*see* page 80 by its size, shape, more measured flight, and its usually pale head, dar belly and whitish, long, broad tail. This species preys mainly on rodent It is a rare migrant to semi-arid areas in east Africa and the numerou putative recent southern African records require confirmation. Its usu wintering grounds lie along the southern rim of the Sahara Desert.

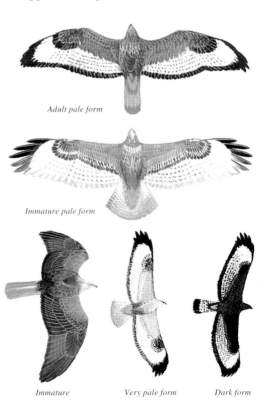

Adult pale form

Immature pale form

Immature   *Very pale form*   *Dark form*

Adult

Immature

79

Jackal Buzzard *Buteo rufofuscus* (152) L 44-53 cm

The adult Jackal Buzzard has a black head and upperparts and a short, bright red tail. The pattern on the underparts is highly variable, and although it usually consists of a black throat, a white upper chest, a rufous lower chest and a black-and-white barred belly, any colour may predominate or be absent. In flight this broad-winged species shows *black underwing coverts*, white flight feathers and a broad black trailing edge to the wing. Adults with white underparts are easily *confused with the Augur Buzzard* (*see* page 82) but show *black underwing coverts* which also distinguish them from the Bateleur Eagle (*see* page 56). The immature Jackal Buzzard is brown above with *rufous underparts and underwing coverts* and a pale, indistinctly barred tail. It can be distinguished from the Steppe Buzzard (*see* page 76) by its shape, rufous colour and heavier body. The Jackal Buzzard has a distinctive tilting flight action when soaring. It is a common endemic to the southern African region and is usually found in hilly country, being most common in regions with high mountains. Rodents, birds and reptiles are its main prey. Its distinctive call resembles that of a black-backed jackal. It often occurs in pairs and usually nests on cliffs and occasionally also in trees from May until October. The Jackal Buzzard was previously considered to be a subspecies of the Augur Buzzard.

Adult

Immature

Adult

Immature

Adult

Immature

81

Augur Buzzard *Buteo augur* (153) L 45-53 cm

The adult has a black head and upperparts, pu[..]
white underparts, and a short, bright red tail. T[..]
male's throat is white and the female's blac[..]
Viewed in flight from below it appears broa[..]
winged and short-tailed, and shows *white und[..]*
wing coverts (except for black crescents on [..]
carpals in the outermost coverts), white flig[..]
feathers, and a broad black trailing edge to t[..]
wing. An all-black melanistic form is not unco[..]
mon in east Africa, especially in high-rainfall areas. The immatu[..]
has brown upperparts, *pale buff underparts with streaking on [..]*
upper chest, pale buff underwing coverts, and a pale, indistinc[..]
barred tail. The paler colour and streaked chest distinguish it fr[..]
the similar immature Jackal Buzzard (*see* page 80) in central Namib[..]
the only place where the two species overlap. The Augur Buzza[..]
has a distinctive tilting flight action when soaring. It is common [..]
mountainous country and even where isolated low hills occur in f[..]
plains. Favourite sites in southern Africa include the northe[..]
Namibian escarpment, the Matobo National Park and the eastern hig[..]
lands of Zimbabwe. Its prey consists mainly of rodents and reptile[..]
The call of this noisy species is distinctly different from that of [..]
Jackal Buzzard. It is often found in pairs and usually nests on clif[..]
and occasionally in trees, mainly from June until October.

Adult male

Immature

Adult male   *Adult female*   *Immature*

Adult

Immature

83

Honey Buzzard *Pernis apivorus* (130) L 54-60 cm

This unusual raptor has a *small round head, a weak bill, loose plumage* and a long tail. The adult has *grey cere and yellow eyes.* The colours of the underparts and underwing coverts are highly variable: the background is white or brown, and can either be plain, barred (typical), spotted, streaked or a combination of these. The male Honey Buzzard has a grey head and grey-brown upperparts, and the female has a brown head with grey around the eyes, and brown upperparts. The flight action is characterized by deep, relaxed wing-beats, and the *wings are held level when soaring.* In flight the *raised head and neck appear long and thin.* The flight feathers are barred and pale with a broad, dark trailing edge, and usually show dark carpal patch. The *tail pattern* is diagnostic with *two dark bars close to the body and a broad, dark tip.* The immature has brown eyes, a yellow cere, a pale rump, and four bars in the tail. It lacks grey on the face and a dark trailing edge to the wing. White-coloured immatures have a black eye-patch. This species is similar to the Steppe Buzzard (*see page 76*), and the brown form can be confused with the immature Gymnogene (*see page 88*). The Honey Buzzard is a rare, non-breeding summer migrant to wooded areas, including plantations of alien trees, and forest edge. It has been recorded with increasing frequency in southern Africa and has recently been found to be not uncommon around Cape Town. This buzzard is a secretive bird and is often attracted to wasp nests.

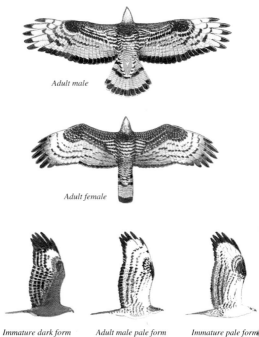

Adult male

Adult female

Immature dark form   *Adult male pale form*   *Immature pale form*

ALAN WILSON

Adult plain form

P. DOHERTY (AQUILA)

Adult barred form

Grasshopper Buzzard *Butastur rufipennis* L 35 cm

This small, slim buzzard is the same size as th
Lizard Buzzard (*see* page 87). It has a dark head
plain slate brown upperparts and distinctive *rufou*
underparts (with streaking on the chest) and win
coverts. The throat is white, the cere, base of th
bill and eyes are yellow, and the legs are pale yel
low. It appears fairly long-legged when perche
In flight it is markedly buoyant and shows a *pal*
rufous patch in the wing. The wing tips and ta
appear noticeably dark; the tail is grey and barred with a broad dark ba
on the tip. The immature Grasshopper Buzzard resembles the adult bu
is pale rufous on the head and neck, has whitish tips to the flight feather
and an unbarred tail. This species
usually inhabits semi-arid woodland and scrub. It often occurs in
small flocks and is a non-breeding
migrant to east Africa from October until April. Its main prey is
insects, occasionally small birds,
which are usually caught from a
low perch, and occasionally on
the wing. It is often attracted to
fires and burnt ground, as well as
to termite and locust emergences.
The Grasshopper Buzzard's numbers have decreased in recent years.

Immature

Adult

izard Buzzard *Kaupifalco monogrammicus* (154) L 35-37 cm

This raptor *resembles a sparrowhawk or goshawk but is stockier* in shape with a *large head, short stout legs and talons*, and a fairly *short tail*. The adult has deep wine-red eyes and a distinctive *pink cere and legs*. The *throat is white* with a contrasting *vertical black stripe*. The head, upperparts and *upper chest* are *plain grey*, and the underparts are barred. In flight it shows a white rump and a black *tail marked with one or two bars*. The immature resembles the adult but is slightly browner and has brown eyes. This species inhabits woodland, especially broad-leaved moist woodland, and subject to marked influxes during some years. Primarily a perch hunter, it preys on insects and reptiles. When hunting, it drops down from perch and flies low to the ground before swooping up swiftly to perch again. A fairly noisy bird, it utters a protracted, melodious whistling call. reeding occurs from May until January, and nests are built in trees.

Adult

dult two-anded tail

Adult

PETER PICKFORD (SIL)

Gymnogene *Polyboroides typus* (169) L 60-66 cm

This unusual raptor has a *small narrow head, bare face, long nape feathers, loose plumage, and long legs.* The adult has a grey head and upper parts, black spots on the upperwing coverts, a grey upper chest, and barred lower underparts. *The face is yellow, flushing red when excited.* In flight the head and neck appear narrow, the wings very broad, and the long, full, black *tail shows a single broad white bar.* The underwing coverts are barred, and the flight feathers are grey with black tips. The immature has a variable brown colouring, a dark face, and bars in the flight feathers and tail. The flight action is slow and buoyant. This species clambers around in trees and on cliffs with wings flapping as it searches for prey such as reptiles and nestlings. It occurs in a wide range of habitats: from flat regions and woodland to mountainous regions and open environments. Breeding occurs from June until December and nests are built in trees and on cliffs. This species has uniquely 'double-jointed' legs, allowing it to explore cavities when hunting.

Adult

Immature

Adult

89

African Cuckoo Hawk *Aviceda cuculoides* (128) L 40 cm

The African Cuckoo Hawk superficially *resembles a sparrowhawk or goshawk but is stockier* and has *longer, broader wings, a dove-like head* and *prominent eyes*. The adult hawk has a *slight crest with a chestnut nape patch*, yellow or red eyes, and a yellow cere and legs. The head, upperparts, upper chest and rump are grey, and the *underparts have broad, irregular chestnut bars*.

Unlike those of sparrowhawks and goshawks, the *wing tips of this species almost reach the tip of the tail* at rest. The Cuckoo Hawk's flight action is sluggish, on long broad wings, and showing a broadly barred tail and *underwing coverts barred with chestnut*. The *immature* bird has yellow eyes, cere and legs, a broad white eyebrow, and lacks the chestnut nape patch of the adult bird; it is brown above and its *underparts are spotted with heart-shaped spots*. A secretive raptor, the Cuckoo Hawk normally occurs in tall woodland and forests, including plantations of alien trees. It shows some movements and is a migrant to coastal areas in east Africa from May until November. Its explosive, whistling call is similar to that of the Grey Hornbill. It feeds mainly on insects and reptiles. Breeding usually occurs from August until March, and its untidy nests are well concealed in tall trees.

Adult

Immature

Adult

90

Adult

Immature

91

Pale Chanting Goshawk *Melierax canorus* (162) L 46-63 cm

This large, long-legged goshawk has a distinctive upright stance. The adult has a red cere, grey upperparts and chest, barred underparts, and red legs. In flight it shows a *white rump*. It is similar to the adult Dark Chanting Goshawk (*see page 94*) but is larger and paler with a pure *white rump and black primaries* which contrast with the white *secondaries* in flight. The secondaries also form a *pale patch in the folded wing* when perched. However, the distribution of the two species overlaps only slightly. The immature Pale Chanting Goshawk is brown with a *streaked chest* and barred underparts. Its eyes are yellow, its cere and legs are yellow or orange and, when viewed in flight from above, a pale window is visible in the primaries. It is paler and browner than the immature Dark Chanting Goshawk, having a more streaked head and chest, a less distinct contrast between the chest and belly, a *white rump* with indistinct rust-coloured V-shaped markings, and upperwing coverts more broadly tipped with buff. The east African subspecies, the Eastern Chanting Goshawk *M.c. poliopterus*, may be a separate species from the southern African race *M.c. canorus*. The adult Eastern Chanting Goshawk is slightly browner, has a yellow cere and orange legs, and darker secondaries compared with the southern African subspecies. Both subspecies usually inhabit open dry regions, such as the Namib Desert, Karoo, Kalahari Desert, and dry woodland. They are common and conspicuous, usually perching on exposed perches such as telephone poles. These noisy birds have a protracted, melodious whistling chant, and prey mainly on rodents, birds and reptiles. They breed from June until December in southern Africa and from February until October in east Africa.

Adult

Immature

HEIN VON HORSTEN

Adult

DARYL BALFOUR

Immature

Dark Chanting Goshawk *Melierax metabates* (163) L 43-56 cm

Like the Pale Chanting Goshawk this large, long legged raptor has a distinctive upright stance. The adult has a red cere, a grey chest and upperparts, barred underparts, and red legs. In flight it shows a *finely barred rump that appears dark at a distance*. The adult *can be confused with the adult Pale Chanting Goshawk (see page 92)* but is smaller and darker, and in flight shows a *dark (not white) rump* and *no contrast between the uniformly grey primaries and secondaries*. However, the distribution of the two species overlaps only slightly. The immature is brown and has yellow eyes, a yellow or orange cere, a *mottled chest*, barred underparts, and yellow or orange legs. It differs from the immature Pale Chanting Goshawk by being darker and greyer and having a less streaked head and chest, a more distinct contrast (gorget) between the chest and belly, a broadly barred rump which appears dark at a distance, and upperwing coverts which are less broadly tipped with buff. This resident goshawk inhabits well-developed woodland. It is fairly common and conspicuous, but its habitat renders it far less conspicuous than the Pale Chanting Goshawk. It is a noisy bird, with a protracted, melodious whistling chant, and preys mainly on rodents, birds and reptiles. Dark Chanting Goshawks nest in trees and breed from June until November.

Adult

Immature

Adult

Immature

95

Gabar Goshawk *Micronisus gabar* (161) L 28-36 cm

This bird superficially *resembles the chanting goshawks (see* pages 92-95) but is *smaller and sparrowhawk-like.* In flight it shows a broad white rump. The adult has brown eyes, a red cere, plain grey upperparts and upper chest, barred underparts, and red legs. The immature has a streaked head, a faint eyebrow, brown upperparts, and *barred underparts with a streaked upper chest.* Its eyes are yellow, its cere is grey or orange, and its legs are yellow or orange. A common melanistic form lacks the white rump and is *distinguished from the melanistic Ovambo Sparrowhawk (see* page 101) by its stockier shape, *distinctive black-and-white barring in the wings and tail, lack of white flecks on the uppertail,* and by the presence of *black scales on the front of the legs.* It also usually differs in cere, leg and eye colour. The Gabar Goshawk is a common resident of woodland, especially dry woodland, and extends further into arid areas along wooded watercourses than do other small sparrowhawks and goshawks. It preys mainly on small birds and sometimes raids weaver nests. Nests are built in trees from August until March in southern Africa and from March until November in east Africa, and are typically festooned with cobwebs. This species is not attracted to alien plantations.

Immature

Melanistic form

Adult

This large sparrowhawk has a *distinctive pied appearance*. The adult has wine-red eyes, a yellow cere and legs, and a *black head, upperparts and rump*. The *underparts are variably marked with black and white*, usually showing a white throat and chest, and a 'waistcoat' of black mottling on the flanks which extends towards the centre of the belly. The immature has a brown head, eyes, upperparts and rump, and black bars on the pertail which are edged with white. The *underparts are marked with ʌg dark streaks* and the background colour is variable, either white or ʃous. In flight the immature shows a distinctive pale window in the maries when viewed from above. A melanistic form occurs which is ʳe except in the extreme south of its range. It is all-black in colour, ɔws *no barring in the wings and tail*, and usually has a white throat. A cretive species, the Black Sparrowhawk occurs in areas with tall trees, ɪluding alien plantations. It is a dashing predator which preys on birds, ƿecially doves, pigeons and francolins. The large nests are built in ɛs, often in alien plantations, and breeding occurs from May until ʰtober in southern Africa, and from March until June and October until ʲcember in east Africa. The fact that this raptor has adapted to plantaˌns and feeds on birds, the numbers of which have increased due to crop ˌrming, has resulted in an expansion of its range in southern Africa.

Melanistic form

Immature

Adult with chicks

African Little Sparrowhawk *Accipiter minullus* (157) L 23-27 cm

This species, the smallest sparrowhawk in t[he] region, has a yellow cere, eyes and legs, a[nd] appears *short-tailed* and compact. The adult b[ird] has grey upperparts and the underparts are barr[ed] from throat to belly. Seen from behind, the tail [is] barred with white spots, and in flight the *ru[mp] shows a narrow white patch*. The immature h[as] brown upperparts, spotted underparts, and unli[ke] the adult, a plain brown rump. This species r[e]sembles the African Goshawk (*see* page 99) but is much smaller with [a] yellow, not grey, cere. The African Goshawk lacks the white rump of th[e] adult Little Sparrowhawk, and the immature Little Sparrowhawk lac[ks] the eyebrow and throat stripe of the immature African Goshawk. Bo[th] the Little Sparrowhawk and the male African Goshawk have distincti[ve]

white spots on the uppertail. This secretive, unobtrusive raptor is a common resident, and is found in forest and well-developed woodland, including plantations of alien trees and especially along watercourses. The African Little Sparrowhawk breeds from August until the end of December and its nests are usually well concealed in trees, including plantations of alien trees. Its prey consists mainly of small birds.

Immature

Adult

DAVE RICHARDS

African Goshawk *Accipiter tachiro* (160) L 36-47 cm

This goshawk has yellow eyes and legs, and a *grey cere*. The upperparts and rump are brown-grey, and the underparts are barred from throat to belly. The female appears distinctly browner than the greyish male and the male shows white spots on the tail when viewed from behind. The immature has a broad pale eyebrow, brown eyes and a *broad brown throat stripe*. Its upperparts are brown and its underparts spotted. Both adults and immatures resemble the respective plumages of the Little Sparrowhawk (*see page 98*) but are larger, with grey not yellow ceres, and lack the white rump of the adult Little Sparrowhawk. The immature Little Sparrowhawk lacks the eyebrow and throat stripe characteristic of the immature African Goshawk. Both the Little Sparrowhawk and the male African Goshawk have white spots on the uppertail. A rare melanistic form of the African Goshawk occurs in central and east Africa. The African Goshawk inhabits forest and tall dense woodland, and preys mainly on small to medium-sized birds and small mammals. In the early morning this secretive bird can be seen performing a slow, high aerial display flight while uttering a far-carrying call of single measured 'clicks'. Its nests are well concealed in trees and it breeds from September until April, but mainly from September until December.

Immature

PETER PICKFORD (SIL)

Adult

Red-breasted Sparrowhawk *Accipiter rufiventris* (155) L 33-40 cm

The Red-breasted Sparrowhawk's *head appears hooded*. Its eyes, cere and legs are yellow, the *upperparts and rump are slate-grey*, the *underparts are plain rufous*, and there are indistinct white flecks on the uppertail. In flight the *rufous underwing coverts* are visible and the rump can appear pale-sided due to the fluffy, pale undertail coverts. The immature has a slight eyebrow stripe behind the eyes, brown upperparts and indistinct streaking or barring on the underparts. It can be distinguished from the similar-looking immature Ovambo Sparrowhawk (*see* page 101) by its yellow eyes, plainer, hooded head pattern, usually less marked upperparts as well as by habitat and distribution.

In South Africa this species inhabits open fynbos, Karoo and high-lying grasslands. Further north in the African continent it is a species of montane regions in mosaics of montane forest and grassland. A relatively conspicuous bird, it hunts on the wing over open country with a distinctive, unstable flapping flight action. Its prey consists mainly of small to medium-sized birds, not bigger than doves. The Red-breasted Sparrowhawk nests from July until December in tall forest trees and alien plantations, especially pines.

Immature

NICO MYBURGH

Adult with chicks

This *slim* sparrowhawk has a *small head, relatively long wings*, and white flecks on the uppertail. The cere and legs of adults may be yellow, orange or red, and the *eyes are wine-red*. The upperparts and rump are grey, and the underparts are barred from throat to belly. The immature has brown eyes, a yellow or orange cere and legs, a broad eyebrow, a *dark ear patch* and a *streaked, pale head*. Its *upperparts are brown with pronounced scale scaling* and its underparts are either rufous or white with indistinct breaking or barring. A *rare melanistic form* can be distinguished from the melanistic Gabar Goshawk (*see* page 96) by its *slimmer shape, indistinct barring in the wings and tail, uppertail flecks*, and the absence of black scales on the legs. It also usually differs in cere, leg and eye colour. The immature bird can be distinguished from the immature Red-breasted Sparrowhawk (*see* page 100) by its eye colour, head pattern, 'scaled' upperparts, as well as by habitat and distribution. The Ovambo Sparrowhawk inhabits a mosaic of open areas and tall woodland, including plantations of alien trees. This secretive raptor is uncommon, except in the Gauteng province of South Africa where it is common. It preys on small birds and nests in trees, especially in plantations of alien trees, mainly from August until November.

PETER STEYN

Immature rufous form

PETER PICKFORD (SIL)

Adult

European Sparrowhawk *Accipiter nisus* L 28-38 cm

The adults of this medium-sized sparrowhawk have *grey upperparts* and their *underparts are barred from throat to belly*. The female appears largely grey-coloured and has yellow eyes with a distinct pale eyebrow stripe. The male has orange eyes, lacks the pale eyebrow and has a rufous wash to the cheeks and underparts. The rump is grey and the grey uppertail is barred with four to five visible black bars without any white markings. The cere and legs are yellow. The immature male is lightly streaked and mottled on the underparts, and the immature female has barred underparts. Immatures have yellow eyes and broad pale eyebrow stripes. This species is a rare non-breeding migrant to the higher-lying regions in east Africa from November until February and is easily overlooked amongst the similar-look-

ing resident sparrowhawks and goshawks. The European Sparrowhawk has no single diagnostic feature separating it from the resident species but the combination of features outlined above for adult males, adult females and immatures should allow its positive identification. This sparrowhawk preys on small birds.

Immature

J.A. SAUNDERS (AQUILA)

Adult

ttle Banded Goshawk *Accipiter badius* (159) L 28-30 cm

This small goshawk is usually the commonest of the sparrowhawks and goshawks in most woodland regions. The upperparts and rump are dove-grey, the underparts are barred from throat to belly, and the cere and legs are yellow. The male has bright red eyes and the female dull orange eyes. Seen perched from the rear and in flight, the *central tail feathers are unbarred*. The *remainder of the tail* feathers are marked with *narrow, black-d-white bars*. The immature has yellow eyes, a faint eyebrow and an *distinct, brown throat stripe*. Its upperparts and rump are brown, and *e underparts have rust-coloured spots* on the upper chest above a rred lower chest and belly. The *tail is nar-*
wly barred throughout but the central tail athers are noticeably darker than the rest of e tail feathers. This common resident curs in a wide range of woodland. It preys lizards and small birds, and characterist-lly swoops up from a low dipping flight to rch in the open. Breeding occurs from ugust until January in southern Africa and roughout the year in east Africa. This ecies usually nests in tall trees, including antations of alien trees.

IAN DAVIDSON

Sub-adult

CHRIS VAN ROOYEN

Adult

Secretarybird *Sagittarius serpentarius* (118) L 138 cm

This large bird of prey looks more like a stork a crane than a raptor. Adults and immatures a similar in appearance, having distinctive and obv ous features such as a red face, a short hooked b an *elongated nape and central tail feathers*, a black leggings. In flight this species can be ide tified by the shape of its head and bill, its sho neck, barred tail, long legs and elongated centr tail feathers. It has a characteristic, brisk stridi gait during which the head is typically tilted downwards as it search for prey. Occurring singly or in pairs, this fairly common resident us ally inhabits open or lightly wooded regions but it is now becomin

increasingly rare in many regions, and is absent in forested and heavily wooded areas. It feeds mainly on insects, rodents, nestling birds and reptiles, especially snakes, which it subdues by stamping on them, usually with the wings held open. The Secretarybird has an eye-catching, undulating display flight, sometimes accompanied by a harsh grating call. It breeds at any time of the year, and nests in the canopies of low trees.

PETER PICKFORD (SIL)

at Hawk *Macheiramphus alcinus* (129) L 45 cm

The adult is black with *two white nape spots* and usually shows a *white throat with a black stripe*, and sometimes a white belly. It has a *slight crest*, large yellow eyes, and *white eyelids and legs*. The small head has a narrow bill with a wide gape. The immature has white underparts with a black band across the belly. In flight this species shows a long tail and pointed wings bent at the carpal joints, which give it a falcon-like appearance. The underwing appears all-black and the tail is barred. This hawk s frequently confused with falcons, kestrels and other raptors which also hunt at dusk. It is even confused with nightjars but is about the same size as the Steppe Buzzard (*see* page 76). A rare raptor, it is restricted to tall, well-developed woodland and forest, including riverine forest and plantations of alien trees, and vagrants wander widely. It s attracted to towns, such as Nairobi and Malindi in Kenya, Mutare in Zimbabwe and Tzaneen in South Africa. The Bat Hawk spends the day

perching in cover in an upright position, and feeds on bats at dusk and dawn. It roosts and nests in pale-barked trees such as eucalypts. Breeding occurs mainly from August until November in southern Africa and from April until June in east Africa.

Immature

Adult

African Pygmy Falcon *Polihierax semitorquatus* (186) L 19-20 cm

This *tiny raptor* is easily overlooked as it resembles a shrike rather than a hawk. It has a red cere, eye-ring and legs, a white face and collar (on the back of the neck), and white underparts and rump. The crown is grey and the tail is black with white spots. The *female's back is rufous* and that of the *male is plain grey*. Viewed in flight from above, it shows black flight feathers with white spots. The immature resembles the adult but is browner, with rusty smudges on the underparts. This falcon is locally common in dry open country. It often hunts insects and lizards from roadside telephone poles. In southern Africa it is mainly found in the Kalahari and Namib deserts and favourite localities include the Kalahari Gemsbok Park in South Africa and the Etosha and Namib-Naukluft national parks in Namibia. In southern Africa it is associated with Sociable Weaver nests, especially along watercourses, and breeds from August until March, making use of the disused nest cavities of the Sociable Weaver. In east Africa it breeds in the nests of White-headed Buffalo Weavers from June until December. Nests occupied by Pygmy Falcons can be identified by the pinkish rim of droppings around the entrance to the nest cavity.

Adult male

Adult female

Immature

Adult male (left) and female (right)

The plumage of this very large pale falcon is variable. The *crown is usually white, sometimes brownish, with dark streaks* and the upperparts are brown with rufous tips to the feathers. The *white underparts have indistinct dark streaks*, especially on the belly and leggings, and the underwing coverts are white with dark brown streaks, especially on the trailing edge of the coverts. This falcon has an indistinct moustacial ripe and a faint dark line from behind the eye to the nape. The cere, e-ring and legs are pale yellow. The tail feathers have diagnostic hite spots, unlike the bars found on the tail feathers of other large falns, but these spots are only visible at close range. The immature is rker above and more heavily streaked on the crown and on the derparts, especially the belly, than the adult. It resembles the immare Lanner Falcon (*see* page 108) but is usually paler above and less avily streaked below, except on the belly. The Saker Falcon is a rare

n-breeding Eurasian migrant to pen areas in the Rift Valley gion in east Africa from ovember until May (mainly ovember) and from March until ay. In Africa this species preys birds and possibly also on nall mammals, lizards and sects. It usually flies close to the round and often hunts near water.

HANNE & DENS ERIKSEN

Immature

CONRAD GREAVES (AQUILA)

Immature

107

Lanner Falcon *Falco biarmicus* (172) L 35-45 cm

The adult of this large falcon has a *rufou coloured crown and nape, pale grey upperpar and plain cream underparts often tinged pink* a spotted on the flanks. The cere, eye-ring and le are yellow. In flight the lightly spotted, crea coloured underwing coverts, and barred flig feathers and tail are visible. The wings are lor broad and blunt-ended, and the tail is relative long. The wing tips reach the tip of the tail wh perched. The immature has darker upperparts, *indistinct tear-shap streaking on the underparts*, a less distinct pale blonde crown, and da underwing coverts. It has pale yellow legs, and a greyish cere and ey ring. This is the commonest large falcon in open areas, but is becomi increasingly scarce in many regions, probably due to agricultural po oning. It can show considerable local movements, for example, imm tures concentrate in the arid western parts of southern Africa duri late summer. These falcons often hunt in pairs and feed on a variety small animals, especially small to medium-sized birds. They bre from June until November and nest on cliffs, pylons and in trees.

Immature

Adult

HEIN VON HÖRSTEN

Immature

Adult

Immature

Peregrine Falcon *Falco peregrinus* (171) L 34-38 cm

This large falcon has a compact body and rela ively short, broad-based, *triangular, pointe wings* which reach the tail tip when perched. Th tail is short. Its fast, shallow, stiff wing-beats ar distinctive, and in flight its dark underwin coverts are visible. Adults have a *bright yello cere*, eye-ring and legs, and a *grey-black hea and upperparts*. The *throat and upper chest a lightly streaked*, and the *lower chest and bel are barred*, creating a two-tone effect on the underparts. The immatur has white nape patches and *discrete streaks and spots on i underparts*. This species differs from the Lanner Falcon (*see page 10* in shape and flight action. Adults and immatures are easily disti guished from adult Lanners by their *darker upperparts, marked unde parts and underwing coverts*, and by their *lack of a broad pale crow* A plain black head, plain dark upperparts, and barred and two-tor underparts distinguish the adult Peregrine from the immature Lanne The immature Peregrine is easily confused with the immature Lanne but the Peregrine has more distinct, narrower markings on the unde parts, and does not have a pale crown. Three subspecies occur in th region. *F.p. minor* is rare and largely restricted to mountainous are although vagrants wander widely. It breeds from August until Decem ber and nests on cliffs and also city buildings, for example, in Cap Town and Nairobi. The larger, paler *F.p. calidus* is a scarce, no breeding Eurasian summer migrant inhabiting a wide variety of ha itats. *F.p. pelegrinoides*, the Barbary Falcon, may be a separate speci and is a rare non-breeding migrant to northern Kenya from Novemb until March. The adult Barbary Falcon resembles the adult Lanne being pale grey above, pinkish below with rufous patches on the nap and ear coverts but it retains indistinct *barring on the underparts* and dark crown. The Peregrine Falcon preys mainly on birds.

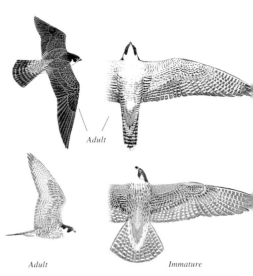

Adult

Adult *Immature*

Adult

Immature

DARYL BALFOUR

DAVE RICHARDS

Red-necked Falcon *Falco chicquera* (178) L 30-36 cm

This small, extensively barred falcon has a slight build, and resembles a sparrowhawk in appearance and habits. The wing tips stop well short of the tip of the tail when perched. The adult has extensive *rufous on the crown, nape and upper chest*, a darker moustachial stripe and facial markings, and a white forehead, throat and cheek patch. The *upper- and underparts are grey and finely barred*, as is *the tail which has a broad black terminal band and a white tip*. In flight the wings appear relatively short and the underwing coverts and flight feathers finely barred. The immature has a darker head, buff nape patches, brown and indistinctly barred upperparts, and lightly barred rufous underparts and underwing coverts. This scarce to locally common resident frequents tree-lined watercourses in the arid Kalahari and Namib deserts in southern Africa and open palm savanna elsewhere in Africa. Favourite localities in southern Africa include the Kalahari Gemsbok National Park in South Africa and the Etosha and Namib-Naukluft national parks in Namibia. This falcon preys mainly on small birds, which are often pursued in level flight. It is attracted to water points, where it hunts birds drinking. Sometimes it hunts in association with the Gabar Goshawk. The Red-necked Falcon breeds from May until October and lays its eggs in disued nests in tall trees and in cavities in palms.

Adult

Immature

Adult

Immature

Adult

113

Sooty Falcon *Falco concolor* (175) L 33-36 cm

This small, slim falcon is uniformly grey w[ith] yellow legs. It has a long tail and wings a[nd] when perched its wing tips extend beyond the [tip] of its unbarred tail. The adult has a yellow c[ere] and eye-ring, a *black spot below the eyes*, a[nd] usually a *small buff patch on the throat*. T[he] plumage is either pale grey with darker, unbarr[ed] flight feathers or dark grey throughout with *bla[ck] shaft streaks*. The immature falcon is grey-bla[ck] and sometimes shows a pale nape; it has a plain white throat a[nd] cheeks, dark moustachial stripe, and *heavy, but poorly defined blotch*-*ing on the buff-coloured underparts*. Seen from below, the flight feath-ers and underwing coverts appear barred, and the *tail indistinct[ly] barred with a broad dark tip*. This species is a locally common, no[n]-breeding summer migrant to the coast of Mozambique and easte[rn] South Africa, and some vagrants wander inland in southern Africa. It [is] usually only recorded in east Africa during migration from April un[til] June, and especially from October until November, and is attracted [to] coastal towns such as Maputo and Durban. Sooty Falcons prey main[ly] on insects, bats and small birds. They are largely inactive during [the] day, hunting only at dawn and dusk.

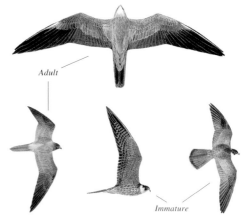

Adult

Immature

W.S. CLARK

Immature (left) and adult (right)

Eleonora's Falcon *Falco eleonorae* (177) L 36-40 cm

This small agile falcon appears highly attenuated in shape, due to its very long tail and long narrow wings. The wing tips do not extend beyond the tip of the tail at rest. The adult has yellow legs, and a *bluish (female) or yellow (male) cere and eye-ring*. It has dark upperparts, a white throat and cheeks, a dark moustachial stripe, and cream to chestnut underparts with dark streaks. Although swift, the flight action is remarkably relaxed, and when viewed from below, a *pale area between the flight feathers and underwing coverts* can be discerned. The *underwing coverts and flight feathers are dark* with distinct markings, contrasting with the pale and barred tail. A rare dark form of this species is grey or black in colour but has indistinct underlying markings. Immatures are browner with more distinct markings, a dark trailing edge to the wing, and *yellow-green legs*. This species is a rare, non-breeding summer visitor to the southeast African coast and it normally winters in Madagascar. It migrates through Kenya between October and November and between April and May. Isolated individuals that occur in Zimbabwe during late summer are possibly on migration to their Mediterranean breeding grounds. This species is active at dawn and dusk, preying on insects and small birds.

Adult female (dark form)

PAUL DOHERTY (AQUILA)

Immature

Adult

Immature

PETER PICKFORD (SIL)

Taita Falcon *Falco fasciinucha* (176) L 28 cm

A compact falcon with a large head, short neck and stocky body. It has *three distinctive rufous markings on the nape* and a white cheek patch edged with rufous. The head and upperparts are grey-black and the *underparts and underwing coverts are plain rufous*, contrasting with the *white throat and cheek patch*. The cere, eye-ring and legs are yellow. The wing tips reach the tip of the tail when perched and in flight it shows short, pointed wings, a short tail and a pale rump. The flight action is fast, swooping and parrot-like, and the bird's shape in flight resembles that of a flying Peregrine Falcon (*see* page 110). The immature is lightly streaked below (sometimes with distinctive spots on the flanks), has pale nape markings, a buff tip to the tail and lacks the pale rump of the adult. This falcon is globally threatened and extremely rare. It inhabits cliffs and gorges in well-developed woodland. Well-known localities for spotting this falcon include the Victoria Falls gorges, the Taita Hills in Kenya and Mount Elgon in Uganda. There are one to two breeding pairs in northeastern South Africa. The Taita Falcon preys on small birds. It nests on cliffs and breeds from August until October in southern Africa and from April until July in east Africa.

Adult

R.R. HARTLEY

Adult

This small brown falcon is slim with long wings and a long tail. The wing tips do not extend beyond the tip of the tail at rest. The cere, eye-ring and legs are yellow. It has grey-black upperparts and head with a dark moustachial stripe and sometimes shows chestnut on the nape. The *underparts are rufous* with faint narrow streaks, and the throat and cheeks are slightly paler. Viewed in flight from below, it shows *rufous, intly streaked underwing coverts and flight feathers*, and a tail that is distinctly barred with rufous. The immature bird is browner above an the adult, with a darker throat and cheeks, and broader streaks elow. It has dark markings on the underwing coverts and a clearly arred tail. In east Africa this species is uncommon in moist woodland nd forest edge but locally common in densely populated and defor-sted highland areas and the Lake Victoria basin. In southern Africa it s rare and restricted to tall woodland in the north and is largely absent uring winter. The African Hobby breeds from August until November southern Africa and from December until October in east Africa, aking use of the disused nests of large birds. It is active at dawn and usk, when it hunts insects and small birds.

Adult

PETER STEYN

Immature

117

European Hobby *Falco subbuteo* (173) L 30-36 cm

This small, black-and-white falcon is easily confused with the female Eastern Red-footed Falcon (*see* page 120). It can be distinguished by its yellow cere, eye-ring and legs, and its solitary habits. Its slight build and long pointed wings give this bird a slim appearance. It has a fairly short tail and its wing tips do not extend beyond the tip of the tail at rest. The upperparts are black. It has a well-defined moustachial stripe, a white throat and white colouring on the cheeks which curls up behind the ear coverts. It often shows a pale collar on the back of the neck. The chest and belly are white, with distinct black streaks which contrast with the *rich rufous vent and leggings*. In flight it shows black spotting on the underwing coverts, and from below the tail and flight feathers appear barred but are unbarred when viewed from above. The immature is browner with a blue-grey cere and eye-ring, broader streaks on the underparts, and lacks rufous on the vent and leggings. This species is a non-breeding summer migrant to southern and central Africa that can be locally common in a wide variety of habitats but is rare in arid areas. It is recorded in east Africa mainly on migration and often in flocks from October until December and from March until April. It is active at dawn and dusk when it preys on insects and small birds.

Adult

DAVE RICHARDS

Immature

Adult

119

Eastern Red-footed Falcon *Falco amurensis* (180) L 30 cm

Both the male and female birds have a *red orange cere and legs*, and a *rufous vent and le[?]gings*. When perched, the remaining plumage the adult male appears plain grey, and in flight shows *white underwing coverts* and a plain gr[?] tail and flight feathers. The female has grey a[?] indistinctly *barred upperparts*, a pale head, wh[?] throat and cheeks, a dark mask through the ey[?] and a dark moustachial stripe. It has white unde[?] parts with black spotting and barring, and in flight it shows black spo[?] on the white underwing coverts. The flight feathers and tail are barre[?] with a broad dark band at the tip of the tail. The immature resembl[?] the female but is browner with more streaked underparts and a le[?] rufous vent. The Eastern Red-footed Falcon is a common, non-breedi[?] summer migrant to grasslands and open woodlands in the eastern par[?] of southern Africa, concentrating mainly in South Africa. It occurs[?] central and east Africa only during migration from November unt[?] December and during April. It has one of the longest distance migratio[?] of any raptor, breeding in Eastern Siberia and crossing the Indian su[?] continent and the northern Indian Ocean to the southern coast of Keny[?] on its way to its southern African wintering quarters. Usually occurrin[?] in flocks, these birds roost communally in tall trees in towns. They fr[?] quently perch on roadside telephone lines, and hover when hunting pre[?] such as insects. Eastern Red-footed Falcons sometimes consort wi[?] Lesser Kestrels (*see* page 124), but have a more easterly distribution[?] moister habitats. This species is considered by some to be a subspeci[?] of the Western Red-footed Falcon.

Adult male

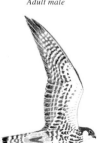

Adult female

Immature

Adult male (above) and female (below)

JOHN CARLYON

121

Western Red-footed Falcon *Falco vespertinus* (179) L 29-31 cm

The male of this species resembles the male Eastern Red-footed Falcon (*see* page 120) but has dark underwing coverts. Both sexes have a *red or orange cere and legs*. When perched, the male appears plain grey with a *rufous vent and leggings*. In flight the male shows *grey underwing coverts* and a plain grey tail and flight feathers. The female has brown-grey *upperparts indistinctly barred with rufous*, a *rufous crown and nape*, a dark mask through the eyes and a dark moustachial stripe; the throat and cheeks are white, and the underparts are pale rufous with faint streaking. In flight the female shows dark spots on the *rufous underwing coverts* and barred flight feathers and tail; the tail has a broad black band at the tip. The immature resembles the female but is paler, has a pale collar at the back of the neck and is browner above and more streaked below. This falcon is a non-breeding summer migrant, mainly to the dry woodlands and Kalahari of Botswana and northern Namibia. It is only very rarely recorded in east Africa on migration from October until November and from March until May; its main migration route appears to be further to the west, through Zaire and Angola. Occurring in flocks, it can be found occasionally in small numbers in the moister east of southern Africa, where it consorts with Lesser Kestrels and Eastern Red-footed Falcons. This falcon often hovers when hunting prey such as insects.

Adult male   *Adult female*

Adult female

Adult male

Adult female

123

Lesser Kestrel *Falco naumanni* (183) L 29-32 cm

The male bird has a *plain blue head and last row of upperwing coverts*, a *plain chestnut back*, buff underparts, and faint spots on the flanks. The *underwing is unbarred white* with a black tip to the wings and faint spots on the underwing coverts. Viewed from above in flight, the *secondaries appear unbarred and bluish*, and the tail blue. The female and immature have a plain brown head, indistinct dark face and moustachial stripe, pale brown barred upperparts, and buff-streaked underparts. In flight the tail appears brown and barred, and the rump greyish. Viewed in flight from below, the underwing coverts are buff with dark spots, and the *flight feathers are pale* and only faintly barred. Both sexes have unbarred primaries when viewed in flight from above, a broad dark band at the tip of the tail, a yellow cere and legs, and diagnostic *white claws*. The main wintering grounds of this non-breeding summer migrant are in the drier grasslands and eastern Karoo of South Africa, although it also occurs regularly in east Africa especially on migration from October until November and from March until April. Although still common in these regions, the Lesser Kestrel's numbers have recently decreased alarmingly and it is now considered to be globally threatened. Lesser Kestrels usually occur in flocks and roost communally in tall trees in towns. They frequently perch on roadside telephone lines and often hover when hunting prey such as insects. They sometimes consort with Eastern Red-footed Falcons (*see* page 120) but have a more western distribution in southern Africa in drier habitats.

Adult male   *Adult female*   *Adult male*

Adult female   *Adult male*

S.C. HENDRIKS

Adult male

BRENDAN RYAN (ABPL)

Adult female

Rock Kestrel *Falco tinnunculus* (181) L 30-33 cm

The Rock Kestrel is the name given to the races of the Common Kestrel that breed in sub-Saharan Africa. These races may constitute a separate species to the Common Kestrel. The Rock Kestrel has a grey and *faintly streaked head*, a dark mark below the eyes, and a yellow cere and legs. I *upperparts are dark rufous with black spots*, and the underparts are rufous with black streaks. The tail has a broad dark tip, and the uppertail is plain grey in the male and barred grey and black in the female. In flight shows white underwing coverts with black spots and barred flight feathers. The female is slightly less grey in colour, while the immature has spotted underparts and is markedly browner on the head, tail and underwing coverts. This is a common resident, except in east Africa where it is fairly uncommon, and is usually found alone or in pairs in a wide variety of habitats, especially in hilly country. The main prey comprises insects, reptiles and rodents. It frequently hovers when hunting and often perches on roadside telephone poles. The Rock Kestrel breeds from June until December and lays its eggs in holes in cliffs, and in trees in the disused nests of large birds. The Common Kestrel occurs in east Africa as a common non-breeding migrant from November until March. Unlike the Rock Kestrel, it is frequently found in flocks. Common Kestrels, especially the females, are paler and less rufous than Rock Kestrels, and female Common Kestrels have brown not grey in their tail.

Adult male   Immature

Immatures

PETER PICKFORD (SIL)

126

PETER PICKFORD (SIL)

Adult male

NIGEL DENNIS (ABPL)

Adult female

127

Greater Kestrel *Falco rupicoloides* (182) L 36 cm

This large *pale brown kestrel* has a bulky head, diagnostic *pale whitish eyes*, and a yellow cere. The *upperparts and flanks* of this bird *are distinctively barred*, the chest is streaked, the uppertail is barred grey and black with a broad dark band on its tip, and the legs are yellow. In flight the wings appear relatively broad. The *underwing coverts are pure white*, the *flight feathers are pale* and faintly barred, the wing tips are black and the rump appears grey. The immature can be identified by its dark eyes, a paler cere, streaked flanks, brown barred tail without the broad dark tip and browner, faintly streaked underwing coverts. This kestrel is resident and common in southern Africa but rather uncommon and local in east Africa. It is found, alone or in pairs, in flat, open dry country such as dry woodland, Kalahari, Karoo and dry grassland. It commonly perches on roadside telephone poles and usually hunts prey such as insects, reptiles and small birds from a perch, hovering relatively infrequently. The Greater Kestrel breeds from July until February in southern Africa and mainly from April until May in east Africa. It lays its eggs in the disused nests of large birds, usually crows, in trees and on pylons.

Adult

Immature

Adult

Adult

Immature

129

Grey Kestrel *Falco ardosiaceus* (184) L 30-33

This very stocky kestrel can be identified by plain dark grey plumage, thick neck, bulky hea stout bill and contrasting yellow cere and leg When perched, the wing tips stop short of the t tip. In flight it shows plain dark grey underwi coverts and faintly barred flight feathers and ta The immature bird resembles the adult but ha pale green cere and browner plumage, especia on the head. This kestrel is uncommon to loca common in tall woodland with open areas and in palm savann Although similar to the Dickinson's Kestrel (*see* page131), the Gr Kestrel is *plainer, darker and stockier, lacks the pale head and rum* and has a *slightly longer tail without the distinct bars and broad da tip*. However, the Grey Kestrel does not overlap with the Dickinson Kestrel in distribution, except possibly in southwestern Tanzania a northern Zambia. This resident species usually hunts prey such insects and reptiles from tall exposed perches.The Grey Kestrel bree from August until October, and usually lays its eggs in disus Hamerkop nests and sometimes also in cavities in trees.

Adult

Immature

Adult

A stocky kestrel, distinguished by its grey plumage and *markedly pale head and mantle*. The remainder of the upperparts are darker than the underparts, and the cere and legs are yellow. The wing tips stop short of the tail tip when perched. In flight this species appears falcon-like, with a *pale, almost white rump*; the underwing coverts are plain grey, the flight feathers barred, and the tail is barred black-and-white with a broad dark band on 's tip. The immature is browner than the adult and has pale barring on he flanks. This species is uncommon to locally common in tall wood-and and palm savanna. A favourite locality is the Kruger National Park n South Africa. Although similar to the Grey Kestrel (*see* page 130), it oes not overlap in distribution with that species except possibly in outhwestern Tanzania and northern Zambia. It preys on reptiles and mall birds, which it hunts from tall exposed perches. It breeds from July ntil November in cavities in tall trees, especially baobabs and palms, nd in disused Hamerkop nests.

Adult

Immature

Adult

131

Barn Owl *Tyto alba* (392) L 30-33 cm

This medium-sized owl has a pale bill, dark eyes and lacks ear-tufts. It can be confused only with the African Grass Owl (*see* page 133) but *is smaller, has a rounder face, paler and more patterned upperparts*, shorter legs, and is less often found on the ground than that species. This common resident inhabits a wide range of habitats but avoids forests. It preys on rodents, insects and small birds, and is subject to large-scale influxes associated with rodent outbreaks. The call is an eerie screech 'shcreee'. It roosts and nests in buildings, holes in cliffs, and Hamerkop nests. Breeding occurs throughout the year, but mainly from February until May in southern Africa.

S.C. HENDRIKS

Adult

African Grass Owl *Tyto capensis* (393) L 34-37 cm

This medium-sized, dark-eyed owl closely resembles the Barn Owl (*see* page 132). It too has a pale bill and lacks ear-tufts. The key differences between the two owls are the African Grass Owl's *larger size, more pointed 'chin', darker plainer upperparts* and *longer legs*. The African Grass Owl is also more likely to be found on the ground than the Barn Owl. This species hunts and nests in wetlands where it occurs alongside the Marsh Owl (*see* page 134). It preys mainly on rodents, but occasionally also takes small to medium-sized birds. One of its calls resembles the Barn Owl's screech, but is quieter and more abrupt. Another typical call is a fast frog-like series of 'clicks'. The African Grass Owl normally roosts and nests on the ground in dense wetland vegetation. Breeding can occur at any time of the year, but usually takes place from February until June in the southern African region. During the last few decades this species' numbers have decreased considerably in many regions due to wetland degradation.

Adult

PETER PICKFORD (SIL)

African Wood Owl *Strix woodfordii* (394) L 30-36 cm

This *richly coloured* owl is medium-sized and lacks ear-tufts. It has a distinctive yellow bill and feet, dark eyes with dark surrounding areas and *white eyebrows*. The *upperwing coverts and shoulders show large white spots*, while the *underparts are heavily barred* with broad chestnut bars. It inhabits forest and tall, well-developed woodland, including riverine forest and plantations of alien trees, and even occur in gardens in such regions. The African Wood Owl preys mainly on insects, but also frequently takes small birds and rodents. It is a secretive and strictly nocturnal bird and is only very rarely seen during the day. The call is a high-pitched 'weh-hoo' or a multi-syllabled 'wohoo-wohoo-dedehoo', which the male and female frequently sing in duet. Breeding occurs mainly from August until November. During this time the African Wood Owl lays its eggs in holes in trees and sometimes in the disused stick nests of other birds.

Adult

PETER PICKFORD

133

Marsh Owl *Asio capensis* (395) L 36-37 cm

This medium-sized owl has dark eyes, a dark bill and small indistinct ear-tufts. It is fairly uniform in colour: dull brown with distinctive *dark area around the eyes and the outer facial disk*. In flight it shows a pale window in the primaries. This common resident inhabits wetlands but also hunts in dry open country. It is usually seen flying in the late afternoon. It quarters the ground and roll-pounces backwards onto its prey in a harrier-like manner. Its prey consists mainly of rodents but it also sometimes takes small birds and insects. The Marsh Owl's call is a harsh croaking 'shquerk' which sounds like canvas being torn. This species often roosts communally and nests on the ground in tall wetland vegetation. Breeding occurs throughout the year but mainly takes place from February until June. The Marsh Owl resembles the closely related Short-eared Owl of Eurasia which is a very rare non-breeding vagrant to Kenya from November until January. The Short-eared Owl is larger than the Marsh Owl, has paler streaked plumage, black tips to the wings and yellow eyes.

Adult

Common Scops Owl *Otus scops* (396) L 13-15 cm

The colour of this small, yellow-eyed owl varies between grey and rufous and there is *little contrast between the upper- and underparts*. During the day the Common Scops Owl roosts in concealed positions, with an upright elongated stance and erected ear-tufts. At night it looks remarkably different when the ear-tufts are flattened giving the head a rounded profile and the body a stockier appearance. This species is common in woodland, especially along watercourses, but is cryptic, highly nocturnal and secretive. Its prey consists mainly of insects but it also sometimes takes rodents, reptiles and small birds. The Common Scops Owl's call is an insect-like, monotonous, measured 'prurp'. Breeding occurs from August until November and its eggs are laid in cavities in trees. The resident African subspecies *O.s. senegalensis*, the African Scops Owl, may be a separate species from the European subspecies *O.s. scops*. The latter is an uncommon, non-breeding migrant to a wide range of habitats in the east African region from November until March.

Adult

A fairly small, grey-white owl with *orange eyes*, black eyebrows, obvious ear-tufts and a *white facial disk with black edges*. It has pale grey upperparts and white underparts, and its plumage is finely streaked with black. There is an indistinct white line through the shoulder. The White-faced Owl inhabits woodland, especially dry thornveld, where it can easily be overlooked. It preys mainly on insects, rodents and small birds. The call is a stuttering, explosive series of hoots 'hu-hu-hu-hu-hu-hu-ugh' which sounds like a single muted hoot at a distance. This common resident breeds mainly from April until October and lays its eggs in the disused stick nests of other birds or in open hollows in trees.

RICHARD VOS

Adult

135

Pel's Fishing Owl *Scotopelia peli* (403) L 63 cm

This owl's large size and *tawny colour* are diagnostic. It has dark eyes, an indistinct facial disk and a rounded head. The upperparts and head are barred with black, whereas the chest is streaked with black, and the belly is marked with indistinct broad bars. The *legs and feet are unfeathered and 'scaly'*. This species is rare and its numbers are decreasing due to the destruction of its natural habitat. It is localized to riverine forest along lowland rivers and flood plains. Its prey normally consists of fish up to 2 kg in weight. The call is a series of deep resonant hoots, 'guh-hu', and wailing screams. Pel's Fishing Owl usually nests from February until June in cavities in tall riverine trees. Favourite localities for spotting this owl in southern Africa are the Okavango swamps in Botswana, the fig-tree forest in the Mkuzi Game Reserve in KwaZulu-Natal and the bridge over the Levhuvhu River in the Kruger National Park in South Africa.

Adult

African Barred Owl *Glaucidium capense* (399) L 20-21 cm

This small, yellow-eyed owl has a distinctive line of white spots along the shoulder and lacks ear tufts. It resembles the Pearl-spotted Owl (*see page 137*), but differs by having a *barred head and upperparts, barred chest and spotted lower underparts, an uppertail barred with buff*, and a larger, rounder head. This species replaces the Pearl-spotted Owl in tall woodland and forest. An isolated and very rare population occurs in thick scrub in the Eastern Cape in South Africa. The African Barred Owl preys mainly on insects, reptiles and small birds. The call is a repeated 'wirow-wirow-wirow' or 'kirow-kirow-kirow'. This rare to locally common resident breeds from September until December, and lays its eggs in holes in trees. The southernmost subspecies of this owl, which occurs in the Eastern Cape, KwaZulu-Natal, Swaziland and southern Mozambique, may be a separate species from populations found further north in Africa.

Adult

136

Pearl-spotted Owl *Glaucidium perlatum* (398) L 17-21 cm

This small, yellow-eyed owl has white spots on the shoulders and lacks ear-tufts. It resembles the African Barred Owl (*see* page 136) but can be distinguished by its *spotted head and upperparts, streaked underparts, an uppertail spotted with white*, and by *two dark patches on the nape*. A common resident in a wide variety of woodlands, it is often diurnal in habits. It frequently perches on telephone poles, characteristically wagging its tail, and has an undulating, woodpecker-like flight. It preys on insects, reptiles, small birds and rodents. The call is a series of explosive whistles 'peu-peu-peu' rising to a crescendo 'peeuu-peeuu-peeuu'. This species breeds in holes in trees mainly from August until November.

DAVE RICHARDS

Adult

Spotted Eagle Owl *Bubo africanus* (401) L 43-47 cm

This large owl has obvious ear-tufts and resembles the rarer Cape Eagle Owl (*see* page 138) but is *smaller, with yellow eyes*, and smaller feet. The *upperparts are finely mottled with grey*, and the underparts, including the *belly and leggings, are finely barred with grey*. A *rufous-coloured form*, particularly common in the dry regions of southern Africa, closely resembles the Cape Eagle Owl. This form has orange eyes, rufous blotched upperparts and dark splotches on the chest, but it retains the *fine barring on the belly*. The Spotted Eagle Owl is a common resident in the region and occurs in all habitats except forest. Its prey consists mainly of rodents, insects, reptiles and small birds. The call is a hooting 'whoo-hoo' with the second note lower than the first, or 'whoo hoo-hoo' with the middle note higher than the other two. The Spotted Eagle Owl nests in cavities in trees and cliffs, and on the ground mainly from July until the end of November.

Adult

Cape Eagle Owl *Bubo capensis* (400) L 48-53 cm

This large, stocky owl has obvious ear-tufts. resembles the Spotted Eagle Owl (*see* page 138) but is larger, has orange eyes, its upperparts are richly patterned with rufous and brown, it has a white throat patch, the chest is heavily blotched forming two dark patches on the upper chest, and the *belly and leggings have very broad bars*. It has larger feet than that species and is more restricted in its habitat, being uncommon and localized in rocky areas, mainly in montane regions. It largely replaces the Spotted Eagle Owl in these habitats. Its prey consists of hares, young hyrax, rodents and small birds. The 'wuh-wuh-hu' or 'wuh-hu' calls resemble those of the Spotted Eagle Owl but are higher-pitched and faster; it also has a diagnostic 'wak-wak' call. The Cape Eagle Owl breeds from May until August in the southern African region and from September until December in the east African region. During this time it lays its eggs among rocks and on cliffs.

Adult

A very large *pale owl with dark eyes, pink eye-lids and indistinct ear-tufts. The pale facial disk is framed with black.* The upperparts are plain grey, whereas the underparts are finely barred with grey. This imposing owl is fairly common in tall woodland and occasionally occurs, and even breeds, well outside its normal range. A ferocious predator, it feeds on large birds and medium-sized mammals up to the size of a ung warthog; hedgehogs are particularly targeted. The 'gu-hu-hu' ll consists of a series of deep discordant, grunting notes. The Giant gle Owl breeds mainly from April until September and lays its eggs disused stick nests and open cavities in trees.

DAVE RICHARDS

Adult

Further reading

Brown, L.H. & Amadon, D. 1968. *Eagles, Hawks and Falcons of the World*. Country Life, Feltham.

Brown, L.H., Urban, E.K. & Newman, K.B. (eds). 1982. *The Birds of Africa*. Vol. 1. Academic Press, London.

Cramp, S. & Simmons, K.E.L. 1980. *Birds of the Western Palearctic*. Vol. 2. Oxford University Press, Oxford.

Del Hoyo, J., Elliott, A. & Sargatal, J. 1994. *Handbook of the Birds of the World*. Vol. 2. Lynx Edicions, Barcelona.

Fry, C.H., Keith, S. & Urban, E.K. (eds). 1988. *The Birds of Africa*. Vol. 3. Academic Press, London.

Kemp, A.C. & Calburn, S. 1987. *The Owls of Southern Africa*. Struik Winchester, Cape Town.

Maclean, G.L. 1993 (6th edition). *Roberts' Birds of Southern Africa*. The Trustees of the Voelcker Bird Book Fund, Cape Town.

Mundy, P., Butchart, D., Ledger, J. & Piper, S. 1992. *The Vultures of Africa*. Acorn Books and Russel Friedman Books, Randburg and Halfway House.

Newman, K.B. 1995 (5th edition). *Newman's Birds of Southern Africa* Southern Book Publishers, Johannesburg.

Newton, I. 1979. *Population Ecology of Raptors*. T. & A.D. Poyser, Berkhamsted.

Pickford, P., Pickford, B. & Tarboton, W. 1989. *Southern African Birds of Prey*. Struik Publishers, Cape Town.

Porter, R.F., Willis, I., Christensen, S. & Nielsen, B.P. 1986. *Flight Identification of European Raptors*. T. & A.D. Poyser, Berkhamsted

Sinclair, J.C. 1987. *Field Guide to the Birds of Southern Africa*. Struik Publishers, Cape Town.

Sinclair, I. & Good, D. 1986. *Struik Pocket Guide Series: Birds of Prey*. Struik Publishers, Cape Town.

Sinclair, I., Hockey, P. & Tarboton, W. 1993. Sasol *Birds of Southern Africa*. Struik Publishers, Cape Town.

Steyn, P. 1973. *Eagle Days*. Purnell, Johannesburg.

Steyn, P. 1982. *Birds of Prey of Southern Africa*. David Philip, Cape Town.

Steyn, P. 1984. *A Delight of Owls: African Owls Observed*. David Philip, Cape Town.

Tarboton, W.R. & Allan, D.G. 1984. *The Status and Conservation of Birds of Prey in the Transvaal*. Transvaal Museum, Pretoria.

Bird organizations

The *Raptor Conservation Group* of the *Endangered Wildlife Trust* dedicated to the conservation of and research on southern African bird of prey. Membership enquiries should be addressed to: P.O. Box 7215 Parkview 2122, South Africa, and members receive copies of *The Journal of African Raptor Biology*. The *Vulture Study Group* similarly dedicated to the welfare of southern African vulture Membership enquiries should be addressed to: P.O. Box 7233 Parkview 2122, South Africa, and members receive copies of *Vultur News*. *BirdLife South Africa* is the leading bird organization in th region. Membership enquiries should be addressed to: P.O. Box 8439 Greenside 2034, South Africa. Members receive copies of the popula magazine *Africa – Birds and Birding* and the scientific journal *Ostric* Membership of these organizations is a positive contribution to th preservation of our magnificent and threatened birds of prey.

Habitat map of southern, central and east Africa

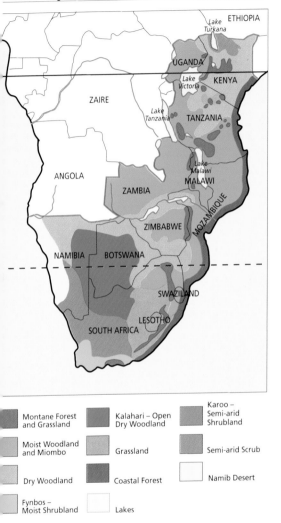

Montane Forest and Grassland

Moist Woodland and Miombo

Dry Woodland

Fynbos – Moist Shrubland

Kalahari – Open Dry Woodland

Grassland

Coastal Forest

Lakes

Karoo – Semi-arid Shrubland

Semi-arid Scrub

Namib Desert

141

Glossary of terms

Alien A species that is not indigenous to an area but has been introduced by man.

Breeding migrant A bird that migrates to an area to breed and then departs to spend the non-breeding season in another region.

Call A vocalization or song of a bird.

Colony Where birds of the same species gather together to breed.

Communal When birds of the same species gather together to rest or sleep (roost).

Diagnostic Refers to an identification feature that is unique to a particular species.

Display Eye-catching behaviour of a bird, usually in flight and often accompanied by vocalizations; used to advertise its presence to its mate or to intruders in its territory.

Diurnal Active during the daytime.

Endemic Restricted to a certain region.

Flight feathers The long feathers in the wing comprising the primaries and secondaries.

Flush When a bird is put to flight.

Form Where a bird species occurs in two or more plumage patterns.

Immature A young bird that has not yet acquired its full adult plumage

Gorget Where the colour and pattern on the upper chest of a bird contrast with those on the lower chest and belly.

Influx Where large numbers of a bird species temporarily concentrate in a particular area, usually because of a super-abundance of food there.

Melanistic A colour form found in some species of which the plumage is all-black.

Migrant A species which moves into and out of a region on a regular seasonal basis.

Nocturnal Active at night.

Non-breeding migrant A bird that migrates from its breeding grounds to another region where it does not breed.

Plumage The feathers of a bird.

Range The area encompassed by the geographical distribution of a bird

Resident A bird that occurs throughout the year in a region and does not undertake migration.

Raptor A bird of prey.

Roost The place where a bird rests or sleeps.

Rufous Reddish-brown colour

Soar A form of flying where a bird holds it wings level and slowly turns in circles without flapping.

Sub-adult The appearance of a bird when it is in transition between the immature and adult stage.

Vagrant A bird found outside the area of its normal distribution.

Index to common names